I0008124

Multidisciplinary
Data
Visualization

Professor Hassan Ugail

Copyright © 2020 Hassan Ugail

All rights reserved.

ISBN: 9798692710437

CONTENTS

ACKNOWLEDGMENTS

This book is a result of many years of research, teaching and learning into the topic of data visualization by researchers and students at the Centre for Visual at University of Bradford, UK. The fundamental and applied research into a topic of the nature described in this book requires both human capital and computational resources. Much of the funding for such resources came from research grants and sponsorship. The list of funders who helped me generously to pursue this work with my team members is exhaustive but undoubtedly memorable. Moreover, it takes a fair amount of dedication and effort to put together a book, and such work often falls outside the regular lines of the day to day academic tasks. As a result, a support base outside the immediate academic environment is essential to complete a book of this nature. I feel blessed to have received enormous support from my dear family members, friends, colleagues and collaborators. Without their support and continued encouragement, this book would not have seen the light of the day. My heartfelt thanks, therefore, goes to all of them. Thank you.

1

INTRODUCTION

It was a fine Sunday afternoon in the month of January in 2020. I was at my home in Yorkshire, England. I usually spend weekends with my family, and as usual, I was sitting with my 4-year-old son in the common room. My son always had a fascination with celestial objects – stars, planets, galaxies and asteroids etc. On this day, he was playing with a planet set I bought for him a few months back. "Mercury, Jupiter, Mars…", he kept uttering in his usual rhythmic voice, picking one at a time from the floor.

Whenever I have a chance to spend some time with him, I make a point of trying to teach him something new. On this particular day, I wanted to show him how the planets in our solar system are ordered. Hence, I brought all the planet pieces together and laid them on the floor in the order in which they appear in our solar system. I made a point to order all in a straight line. Though the chances of all the planets in our solar system lining up are so rare, on this occasion, I chose to line them on the floor, to explain my son, the order, from the sun, of the planets in our solar system.

The above narrative may appear to be straightforward. However, it is an example of a good visualization - in this case, my choice to teach my son how the planets are arranged in the solar system. To do that, I did choose to line them up in a straight line. This simplifies the process, but it enhances his visualization. It emphasizes the story and the crucial information I have decided to convey to a 4-year-old. Many of the effective data visualization strategies adopt similar approaches. And, visual thinking is the heart of compelling visualizations.

Visual thinking and remnants of data visualization probably go way back to the beginning of human civilization. The ancient paintings covering the interior walls and ceilings of the cave of Lascaux in southwestern France is believed to be over 17,000 years old. In them, our ancestors have created powerful visual representations of the stellar data or information such as the location of stars. The clay tokens found in Zagron in southeastern Turkey dating back 4000 BC is another good example of early human visualization. In those tokens, our ancestors have tried to represent numbers of animals with symbols, e.g. one token for a sheep, a different token for ten sheep and another token for ten goats etc.

Fast forward to the more recent human history. From Leonardo Da Vinci to Albert Einstein, even recent human history appears to be littered with visual thinkers. Da Vinci was a master of visualization. He believed in simplicity. He believed in knowing an entity or a phenomenon well enough to be able to express it in visual form from memory. As the 6000 of his unique drawings clearly reveal, Da Vinci believed in the lack of clutter, bold strokes and the use of symmetry. These are hallmarks of compelling data visualizations. As for Einstein, from the age of 16, he started visually imagining how light travelled. He asked bold questions such as "what would it feel like to be riding on a beam of light", which required mental visualization. From the very beginning, Einstein was predominantly carrying out thought experiments where visualizations formed a great deal of his thought process. It is these thought experimentations and mental visualizations that helped him to come to the conclusion that the speed of light must be a constant which of course ultimately revolutionized our understanding of the universe.

Good visualizations reside in a novel dimension of communication. A good visualization can turn the words of verbal communication into a simple chart conveying an additional dimension of conversation aiding to the decision-making process. A good visualization is powerful enough to extract knowledge from copious volumes of data. Visualization, though extremely important, is often a topic which has not been, until very recently, taken seriously. It is usually a side topic which students and professionals are generally required to learn by themselves and hence usually does not form to be part of a formal curriculum.

At this point, I want to share a story from my numerous engagements with many motivated students on a data visualization module I have been teaching over many years. The module is part of the taught masters course in Big Data and Technology, which we offer at the University of Bradford. Every year, I throw my students a task which involves a selected dataset and a predefined question which they must answer based on the dataset. I do not prescribe any specific method or tool for them to analyze the dataset and plot their visualization charts. Though the students are interested in data science, they come from diverse backgrounds ranging from creative design to computational modeling. After teaching them sufficient background on the basic principles of visualization, I throw my problem at them to examine the lens through which they see the problem and the image they present back to me as their most meaningful visualization that they believe answers my question. Interestingly, each of the students come up with an innovative form of visualization ranging from Excel bar charts to sophisticated cluster analysis.

Just like an apple cannot be directly compared with a pear, it is a daunting task to compare and contrast different techniques of visualization as a solution to a given problem. In this sense, data visualization is a recipe that combines, creative thinking, design, science, mathematics and domain knowledge. And at the end of each term what my students are most stunned about is the fact that they need to be thorough with all these elements for them to be able to create meaningful visualizations.

Often in my teaching, in data visualization, there are key messages I do communicate with my students. It is essential to think of the message or messages to be communicated through the visualization than the specific method that one wants to adopt. For example, a pie chart or a bar graph can easily communicate the same message. Taking extreme care to deliver an accurate message to the audience and avoiding any misleading information is essential too. For example, seeing the relationship between two quantities on a line graph may prompt one to think that correlation means causation and such notions must be avoided at all costs. In a visualization, one must summarize a complex and often a big dataset in just one picture. Excellent use of space, graph types, colors and shades are crucial. And, of course, a good understating of the technical details of how to produce charts, how to undertake statistical comparisons and how to plot the relations are fundamental.

About this Book

It does not take much for one to find out that there currently exists much-celebrated literature in the field of data visualization. This text is not intended to be yet another book on data visualization. As the title of this book suggests, an important keyword to note is "multidisciplinary". I wanted to highlight this. I wanted to celebrate how rich the field of data visualization can be by drawing reports, case studies and examples from a diverse field. I wanted the reader to have a recipe book of visualization, which is diverse and which will highlight potential visualization solutions for the era of information and data explosion we are currently witnessing. As the complexity of data and information becomes staggering in almost any field we can think of – from science, engineering to economics – visual interpretation is becoming ever so crucial. As a result, understanding the principles and techniques of data visualization in a multidisciplinary setting has become decisive as well as essential.

Talking of the multidisciplinary angle of data visualization, let us take a brief look at the field of data visualization in healthcare. We can start with a well-known visualization that helped establish the causality of cholera in Dr John Snow's map of cholera deaths in Broad street in London plotting the number of fatalities as bar graphs (an example discussed later in this book). Another equally great health-related visualization is the rose diagram showing the causes of mortality in the army during the Crimean war by Florence Nightingale (also discussed later in the book).

By its very nature, healthcare is a critical industry involving multiple stakeholders. They include patients, their family members, doctors, care providers, policymakers, and private enterprises who provide services to governmental caregivers such as the National Health Services of the UK. Data visualization plays an essential role in providing tools to communicate with a broad set of audiences. There are some significant areas where data visualization can help in decision making.

Global health priority setting can be seen with regard to the United Nation's Sustainable Development Goal on health, the SDG3. The SDG3 is to "ensure healthy lives and promote well-being for all at all ages". A number of indicators have been developed to monitor progress on a number of health and well-being indices. The development of a multi-dimensional index is used to provide a comparative snapshot for the performance of a country. Maps produced by Public Health England, for example, showing disease patterns such as diabetes and obesity, which clearly show a strong link between multiple deprivations and the prevalence of such diseases. Mapping of pathways and interventions can show the complex contributory factors to childhood obesity. In the healthcare sector, large amounts of patient data are available, and only a tiny proportion of this data has been analyzed only scratching the surface of the sphere of benefit. Examples of such studies may be on predicting preterm birth risks or predicting responses to chemotherapy in breast cancer patients where mapping the various relationships that exist may prove to be crucial.

In the world of economics, business and marketing, visualizations are increasingly becoming essential. Business intelligence, as they call it, provides mechanisms to analyze large quantities of data and provide the results visually to the managers, corporates as well as customers to make business-critical decisions. Today, we need efficient and effective visualization methods and tools for making decisions in very short spaces of time. Often, patterns and trends within large datasets in text form will get unnoticed. However, with the right choice of analysis and visualization tools, such text-based data becomes a source that provides more significant insights and powerful drivers for making optimum decisions. Harnessing the power of data and developing efficient dashboards for visually analyzing the data as opposed to using gut feelings is something many sensible bosses of companies have opted for. Such tools help keep the line managers to be in a position for making confident decisions keeping the entire workforce motivated.

Moving to the topic of climate change – one of the biggest threats faced by humanity today – again, data analysis and visualization is an essential entity one must consider. Global warming, urban and agriculture pollution, wildfires, and other factors that result in extreme climate changes are the harsh realities of the present world that poses a significant threat to human existence. The sustainability of life demands immediate and daring action. The continuous monitoring of natural resources and climate change could guide us in the right direction. For example, studying the difference in the chemical and physical composition of the water over time can tell us much about the changes in climate. The trend in water pollution over many years can be studied and shown in the form of charts. Such visualizations can tell many convincing stories and present hard facts that will be difficult to deny. It can provide with enough points for the decision-makers and legislators to develop and enforce the right type of regulations, saving the planet and ultimately saving humanity.

There are many areas a book of this nature must touch upon. We are currently in an era in which data and information are exponentially growing. We are quickly becoming data rich but knowledge poor. It is crucial to understand ways and strategies to handle big data and convert them into meaningful visualizations. Insights from datasets have to be often communicated to a diverse range of clients – from professionals to lay customers. To convey the right messages to an audience, the choice of methods and techniques must be appropriate. Today, we often have to work in multidisciplinary settings with people from diverse backgrounds. In such environments, terminology takes a critical position. Knowledge of the right terminology and understanding that the terminologies may be interpreted in more than one way within a group of people with diverse backgrounds must be appreciated. These are some of the crucial elements of visualization this book highlights.

This book starts off with a gentle introduction to data visualization, highlighting the importance and the relevance of data visualization. The question of why we must embrace data visualization is answered. Data visualization is an art as well as a science. The book is dedicated to explaining this in detail. Key elements of good visualizations are discussed. The art of choosing the charts, the colors and the shades to decorate the visualizations are discussed in detail. There exist very many methods and techniques for data visualization. The book highlights the common methods and techniques for data visualization – ranging from simple charts to complex maps. The aim here is to expose to the reader the depth and breadth of the methods and techniques that are available. Equally, the reader will be exposed to the varieties and types of software tools available to create visualizations. A crucial part of this book is to provide numerous multidisciplinary examples. A whole chapter in this book is dedicated to delivering multidisciplinary data visualization examples from a wide variety of backgrounds. Reading and understanding these examples will help the user to appreciate the mindset and the methodologies one must adopt in tackling significant data visualization challenges.

2

A VISUALIZATION IS WORTH A THOUSAND DATA POINTS

You find yourself in a meeting with your colleagues discussing an important issue. Each of you fervently raising their views, it becomes challenging to be able to agree on important definitions, preferences and priorities. As they often do, it soon brews into a conflict with a dim outlook of reaching unanimity. And that is when the smartest person in the room will stand up and walk to the whiteboard. On it, he would calmly draw a visual to interconnect the myriad of ideas and arguments. The commotion dies as quickly as it began because a visual aid has a far better potential to reach a consensus. Words, they try, but a picture does not have to.

The Human Brain is Wired for Visualization

Two third of the human brain is involved in the processing of visual information. As a matter of fact, hundreds of millions of neurons in the brain - taking up around 30% of the cortex - are designated for visual processing. In contrast to this, the neurons responsible for the senses of touch and hearing, for example, take up around 8%.

The human brain has evolved to handle volumes of visual data we encounter. The process of visualization starts with the retina - which contains 150 million light-sensitive rod and cone cells. By the way, the retina itself is an outgrowth of the brain. Through this complex mechanism, the brain processes visual stimuli in the form of colors, shapes and sizes.

The brain also has mechanisms for filling information to correct blind spots, distorted information and erase irrelevant data. In fact, one of the fantastic feats of the human brain is its extraordinary ability to focus on individual tasks and filter out distractions selectively. Though the brain is continuously bombarded with information from the senses, it has the remarkable power of varying the level of vigilance to such information, e.g. allowing to focus on a pictorial graph or a listening to one conversation but not another.

Figure 1.1: The brain has a higher capacity to engage in visuals.

Despite the impressive visual information processing power of the human brain, its functionality can be severely limited, especially within multiple cognitive domains presented with time constraints. Behavioral research has highlighted the existence of significant bottlenecks in the brain for information processing that can cripple our ability to perceive the visual world consciously. For example, for visual perception tasks, the amount of domain-specific information that can be processed during a certain period of time is estimated to range between 2 and 60 bits per second. Thus, a certain degree of cognitive control or simplification of the stream of information to the brain is essential in order to be able to make the correct and optimal decision.

Figure 1.2: The brain also has a superior capacity to focus its attention where it is needed.

William Shockley, the co-winner of the Nobel Prize for Physics in 1956 for his exceptional work in the development of the modern transistor, could highlight this fact to us too well. It was in 1948 that his colleagues John Bardeen and Walter Brattain invented the point-contact transistor. That was in Shockley's absence, and he got so upset about the entire matter that he huddled in a hotel room for days thinking about it and trying to work out a superior solution than his colleagues. Later, when he came out, he had with him an entire design template for a junction transistor which was far more remarkable. His work is much credited and considered to be the key to modern electronics.

As of the year 2019, it is estimated that humanity is in possession of 40,000,000,000,000,000,000,000 bytes or 40 trillion gigabytes of digital data. That is many million folds more than the size of the documents in the US Library of Congress, and that is 40 times more bytes than there are stars in the universe. And, more interestingly, 90% of this data has been created in the last two years alone. Man's need for ever-growing automation and the consequent rise in technology has meant that data and information are being generated at an unprecedented rate, and it is only on the rise. Such quantitative forms of data require mechanisms, methods and techniques to turn them into suitably qualitative experiences, especially in the visual spectrum.

Visualization Reveals Trends and Patterns in the Data

It was in the unusually cold morning of Tuesday 28th January 1986 that the space shuttle Challenger launched from Cape Canaveral, Florida into space. The launching spectacle was watched by millions of people and, 73 seconds into the launch, those who were watching were horrified to witness the explosion of the spacecraft as it was blasting into pieces. The solid boosters of the Challenger were to be blamed for this disaster, which exploded plunging the shuttle into the Atlantic Ocean, resulting in the instant death of all the crew on-board. There is sufficient evidence to believe that a significant failure of this routine mission can be at least partly blamed to the lack of sufficient clarity in the visualizations presented to the decision-makers who were in charge of deciding whether to go ahead with the launch or not.

A mechanism in the shuttle called the O-rings is used to seal the bottom of rocket boosters. The prime purpose of the O-rings was to prevent hot combustion gases and particles from escaping into the interior of the booster. It is known that these O-rings fail at particularly cold temperatures and the outside thermal reading on the day of shuttle launch was particularly low, at 31 degrees Fahrenheit.

Motor	MBT	AMB	O-Ring	Wind (MPH)
DM - 4	68	36	47	10
DM - 2	76	45	52	10
QM - 3	72.5	40	48	10
QM - 4	76	48	51	10
SRM - 15	52	64	53	10
SRM - 22	77	78	75	10
SRM - 25	55	26	29	10

Blow-By History
SRM – 15 Worst
• 2 Case Joints (80°), (110°) ARC
• Much worse visually than SRM - 22

SRM – 22 Blow-By
• 2 Case Joints (30-40°)

SRM – 13A, 15, 16A, 18, 23A, 24A
• Nozzle Blow-By

Figure 1.3: Typical data presented during discussions in preparation for the shuttle Challenger launch (Vaughan 1996).

Figure 1.3 shows typical data from a document that the engineers presented to their superiors to provide information about shuttle conditions. As one can imagine, the data shown in Figure 1.3 does not convey important information in an understandable way. In fact, apart from showing raw data in a tabulated form, it does not convey any insight into the condition of the shuttle. However, to say the least, it was difficult for NASA engineers and decision-makers to interpret.

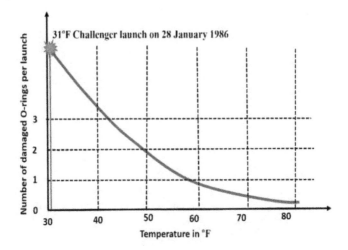

Figure 1.4: A visualization showing the condition of the O-rings with temperature. (Graph adapted from Tufte 1997).

On the other hand, as proposed by Edward Tufte, Figure 1.4 shows similar data in a graph format where it clearly shows the relation between temperature and the condition of O-rings (Tufte 1997). The visualization in Figure 1.4 is clear and succinct. Had the data been presented in this format to the decision-makers, perhaps the launch would have been postponed and lives would have been saved.

Visualization Reveals the Underlying Connections Between Variables

In August 1854, London, England was a dire place. With a terrible outbreak of deadly cholera, the Soho area of central London was deadly. With 10% of the population getting infected every single week, Londoners were fleeing the city, and the outbreak had no prospect of being contained.

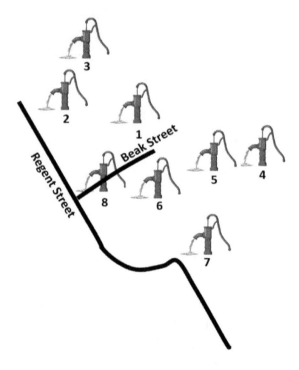

Figure 1.5: Description of the position of the prominent water pumps in London Soho area in 1854.

The dominant theory on the outbreak and the propagation of cholera the experts had at the time was based on the

Miasma Theory. This theory suggested that the disease is being spread through the air and is contagious. Given the musty nature of the central London environment at the time, this was a plausible theory and many, including highly regarded scientists and medical experts at the time, believed it.

However, there was one Londoner, called Dr John Snow, who had a different conviction. He postulated that the disease was being spread through water and the pumps located at key points around the Soho were the main culprit. Dr Snow was well known for his medical expertise, especially for his work in anesthesiology. In fact, he was the anesthesiologist to the Queen during the birth of her eighth child. However, his well-documented expertise in the field and his celebrated standing in the community did not convince the other experts and the learned people that cholera transmits through the water.

Dr Snow's approach to understanding the problem was to track the hospital and public records and link them on the use of the water from various pumps – all shown in a visual form, overlaid on the map of Soho. Figure 1.5 shows the description of the position of the prominent pumps in London Soho area in 1854. Dr Snow demonstrated that those who lived near the specific contaminated water pumps were most likely to acquire the disease and die. For example, in one particular case, he noted that the owner of a coffee shop on Broad Street served glasses of water and recorded a number of those customers contracted cholera (Johnson, 2006). He also diligently investigated groups of people who did not acquire cholera and has shown that they did not use water from those specific pumps. Dr Snow's map with the visualization of the cholera outbreak was instrumental in communicating the information to a mass audience about how the deadly disease was spreading. Despite much resistance from the eminent scientists, medical professionals and other learned people of the time, Dr Snow was eventually able to convince them of his theory of cholera transmission.

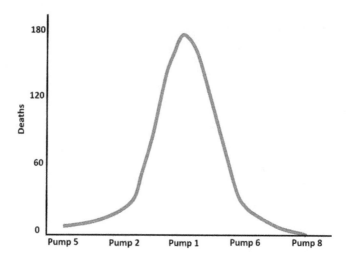

Figure 1.6: An enhanced visualization of the cholera outbreak in the Soho area in 1854 - inspired by Dr Snow's original data collection and visualizations, (Johnson, 2006).

Figure 1.6 shows a visualization which takes a rather close look at the distribution of the deaths within the Soho area in London in 1854. In his original map-based visualization, Dr Snow showed that the highest number of deaths per 50 meters occurred around Pump 1 on Broad Street. The enhanced visualization in Figure 1.6 shows the number of deaths every 5 meters within 100 meters around each pump. It shows that out of 8 pumps considered only 5 were highly contaminated with cholera. It further demonstrates that the closer the residents to the Pump 1, the more likely they were to contract the diseases and the more likely they were to die.

Visualization Helps to Enhance Storytelling

Storytelling is a central human experience. Many of the significant events in your life, many of the memories you cherish, and many of the conversations you recall would have stories in them. As the brain detects visual forms, such as faces, flowers or vehicles, it puts compelling narratives into apparent visualizations. Moreover, a great visualization may help act as a medium to separate useful signals from the unnecessary noises in the stories. Let's try to illustrate this by way of an example.

According to the World Health Organization, every single day, some 830 women die while giving birth to a child. In this age of significant technological advancements, it is unfathomable that so many lives are lost during childbirth. The United Nation's Sustainable Development Goal (SDG) 3 which focuses on health and well-being aims to reduce the global maternal mortality to less than 70 per 100,000 live births by the year 2030 (WHO, 2016). In 101 countries, the Maternal Mortality Ratio (MMR) is less than 70 per 100,000 live births, but in 83 countries, it is presently more than 70 per 100,000 live births. In some 16 countries, in fact, the MMR figures are more than 700 deaths per 100,000 live births, i.e., ten times the WHO target figure. A common perception is that MMR will be high in low-income countries. However, the 83 countries with MMR higher than 70 include middle-income countries and emerging economies such as India, Indonesia and South Africa.

Using the data from various websites of the United Nations and the World Health Organization for 186 countries for the period 1990 to 2015, one could easily visualize the situation of MMR graphically. An example is shown in Figure 1.7.

There are a number of interesting observations one could draw from such a visualization. They include,

1. for most countries, MMR appears to be declining,
2. for a small number of countries such as Myanmar, Timor-Leste, and Lao PDR, the MMR seems to have gone up between 2000 and 2010 before coming down again,
3. for some countries especially those in Europe, the rate of MMR has been consistently low since 1990,
4. and the vast majority of the countries with MMR more than 100 is in Africa but as noted countries from other regions such as Paraguay, Bahamas, India, Lao PDR and Afghanistan also have MMR higher than 100.

Further exploration of the graph may lead us to understand the causes behind the observations above. For example, in the case of Sierra Leone, the MMR figure reached a peak of 2900 per 100,000 live births in 1994. It also has the most dramatic fall, to 1360 per 100,000 live births in 2015, though it still exceeds the SDG's target of 70 per 100,000. The steep rise in MMR can be explained due to the impact of the civil war in Sierra Leone at the time.

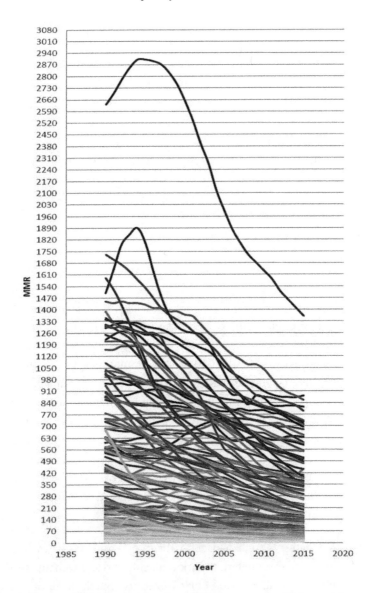

Figure 1.7: Line graph showing the trend of Maternal Mortality Ratio for various countries from 1990 to 2015.

Discussions

Data visualization is a human-centric activity. We need data visualization because the information in visual form is more accessible for us to understand and to grasp. A visual summary of a given set of information brings out the patterns, trends and outliers in the data. Generating visual summaries from information is a natural mode at which the human brain operates. Though without any form of visualization, one may still be able to pull insights from the data, it may still be difficult to communicate such information without proper channels of visualization.

Over the last decade, the abundance of big and complex data generated has grown exponentially. However, the human brain and our visual system never have evolved even in minuscule terms over this short period of time. Hence, the human brain is not geared to understand, process and make sense of such copious volumes of data. Unlike computers, humans do not have the memory capacity to take in such full volumes of data and such information load all at once. Unlike computers, the human brain has not evolved to deal with copious amounts of quantitate data at varying scales. Turning quantitative data into qualitative visualizations is, therefore, needed to provide the salient headlines while dealing with our evolved but inefficient brain for this task.

Mechanisms such as dashboards in cars and on planes help users see essential information quickly and show changes to vital elements over time. However, too much detail or too little context obfuscates and hinders the understanding and is a delicate balancing act which requires more thought in regards to human perceptions to aid decision-making. Visual perceptions may bring powerful visual cues which can complement words and data, and it is critical to wield a user's unconscious attention and tell a convincing story. Overall stories are helpful aids to simplify and amplify the messages which are embedded deep within the data.

In short, data visualization is a particularly human process which helps us to grasp and decipher the meanings in the quantitative world of data. With the help of appropriate methods, techniques and tools, such quantitative data can be turned into qualitative visual forms from which humans can make better decisions and take appropriate actions.

References

E. Tufte, "Visual Explanations: Images and Quantities, Evidence and Narrative", Graphics Press, Cheshire, CT, (1997).

D. Vaughan, "The Challenger Launch Decision", University of Chicago Press, Chicago, IL, (1996).

S. Johnson, "The Ghost Map: The Story of London's Most Terrifying Epidemic – and How It Changed Science, Cities and the Modern World", Riverhead Books. ISBN 1-59448-925-4, (2006).

WHO, "Trends in Maternal Mortality 1990-2015", WHO, Geneva, (2016).

3

PRINCIPLES OF EFFECTIVE DATA VISUALIZATION

Data visualization is the effective communication of complex and qualitative ideas with precision, clarity and efficiency. A useful visualization allows one to see a picture which may go unnoticed if the data had not been appropriately visualized. Any complex dataset contains a multitude of information – and, if the data is not appropriately visualized, then the trends, patterns and correlations can go unnoticed. Visualization allows aspects of data to be highlighted, and in many ways, tells a story.

A Brief History of Data Visualization

Like many other fields, data visualization has a long history.

Pre – 17th Century: The concept of visualization can be seen even before the 17th century, especially in the use of geometric diagrams and maps used for navigation. By this time, methods for precise observation and measuring physical quantities were very well established. During this time, the world saw the creation of the first world map, a form of visualization where information is projected onto a spherical body. Even the use of the proto bar graph was present before the 17th century alongside the logic of the relationship between a tabulated and graphed value.

Towards the end of the 15th century, Leonardo Da Vinci used rectangular coordinates to analyze the velocity of the falling object.

17th Century: During this time period, people were particularly focused on solving problems related to time, distance and space. During this century, we saw the birth of probability theory and demographic statistics. Some of the inventions and discoveries during this time include the pantograph, first print of astronomical pictures, the invention of logarithms, first calculator and the co-ordinate systems for mathematics. Notably, the mathematician Pierre de Fermat discovered that the equation $f(x, y) = 0$ represents a curve in the xy plane, and the graph for the continuous distribution functions came into existence.

18th Century: During this period, people were focused on developing the pre-existing concept of a map, iso-lines and contours for mapping of physical quantities. Initial attempts were made to map medical data. The graphs of functions and measurement errors were introduced. During this century, economic and political data began to be collected, and visual forms were beginning to be utilized to show the data. The technological advancements during this century allowed for ease of creation and reproduction of visual print forms, due to the invention of the color printer.

The Early 1800s: The first half of the 19th century saw the beginning of 'modern data graphics' systems. The previous creations and developments of techniques and design forms led to a growth in statistical graphics as well as thematic mapping. This period also saw the introduction of bar charts, Pie charts, histograms, line graphs, contour plots and time series charts.

The Late 1800s: This is somewhat the 'golden age of graphics'. During this time, throughout Europe, statistical offices were established. Here the importance was placed upon numerical data for social planning and transportation. Notably, statistical theories were used to make sense of the data. During this time period, we also saw the emergence of three-dimensional surfaces and slices.

The Early 1900s: The early 20th century saw the use of graphical methods in sciences such as engineering, biology and medicine. Practical aids for graphing were developed, and new ideas for multidimensional data visualization were introduced. The advancement in computers and computational power helped to support new progress in data visualization.

The late 1900s: The end of the 20th century saw the processing of data by computers at an unprecedented scale. It allowed graphic forms to be constructed by computer programs and to be displayed via high-resolution graphics pipelines. This period also saw more commercial entities, such as software developers and vendors, venturing into the world of visualization. The result was the development of standardizations for visualizations and the introduction of various software packages for data analysis and visualization.

The 21st Century: In the 21st century, we have highly developed tools and knowledge to visualize the data that is being produced at an unprecedented rate. The ride-hailing company Uber is a good example to highlight the sophistication of data visualization we use today. Uber uses mapping techniques to visualize map data such as street segments, building structures and layers of abstract information like pickups and drop-offs. It also uses geospatial data exploration. These visualizations can be used to compare, for example, morning and evening trips to see which times are most popular and which routes and destinations are used at these particular times.

Figure 2.1: An example of how Uber uses effective mapping techniques to enhance visualization.

They can be used to see correlations between journeys. They use this to study travel patterns. As is evident from their website, Uber dedicates a lot of its focus to data exploration, creating libraries and tools which would effectively allow for the visualization of the data, and also allow the end-users to interact with the system. Uber uses the idea of storytelling when it comes to visualizing data. For example, they recently created a visualization that explores how uberPOOL can have an impact on making transportation in cities much more efficient. It shows traffic per each street segment and demonstrates POOL's ability to make cities smarter by reducing traffic.

Today, creating an excellent visualization requires thought and expertise with a clear understanding of the problem domain and the data to be visualized. With a wide array of methods, techniques and tools to choose from, the overall goal of data visualization is to communicate the patterns and connections in the data as succinctly as possible. Therefore, knowledge of the problem domain and understanding of the target audience is essential for effective data visualization. One must equally be aware of the basic principles to communicate a message effectively. Thus, determining the target audience and the right method or tool, one can convey the information better to the target audience.

A Good Visualization Tells and Effective Story

Storytelling is fundamental to human communication. We can infer good stories well before we are taught how to read or write. Even more so, today, the act of storytelling has become a massive part of our culture. Movies, news, books and architecture alike are highly influential elements of our everyday life in which storytelling plays a central role. Throughout the long history of data visualization, the use of storytelling is a key characteristic in order to convey the meanings and viewpoints effectively. Let's depict this by way of some examples.

Minard's Map: In the year 1812, Napoleon Bonaparte - arguably the most powerful leader that Europe has seen - was doing pretty well for himself. At the time, the Russian leader Czar Alexander was becoming too powerful, which created unease with Napoleon. He decided to attack Russia with a massive army of over 400,000 soldiers. Though Napoleon's soldiers outnumbered the Russian troops, the Russians had a different strategy. As the attacks went on, the Russians kept on retreating, and while doing so, they ensured that everything is destroyed from the land as they retreated so that Napoleon's army was left with essentially barren land. This meant Napoleon's army had to endure major hardship along the way and eventually, much of his army was to die due to the lack of sufficient food, severe winter weather conditions and unmanageable diseases.

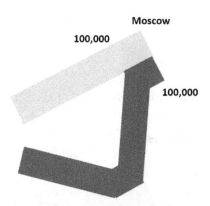

Figure 2.2: Minrad's map showing the rate at which soldiers in the Napoleons army were joining and leaving – the darker shade represents the rate of desertion, and the lighter shade represents the rate of joining.

Charles Minard - a French civil engineer well known for his visualization work at the time - cleverly depicted the story of the disastrous loss suffered by Napoleon during the Russian campaign. In his visualization, Minard used a thick band to show the size of the army on the specific locations as the war progressed. As illustrated in Figure 2.2, with a band graph depicted for loss of lives, location, as well as other key information, Minard was able to tell a compelling story.

Minard's map, partly shown in Figure 2.2, primarily tells the story because it conveys that information in a simple format so as it can be easily processed by humans. Suppose if we imagine that we were to have this information in the form of a table, in order to interpret this data, it may be hard for many of us to understand because all the eyes would see would be a bunch of numbers. Now, we are not saying that statistical data in the tabular form does not tell a story. However, comparatively speaking, such a story will not be processed easily and effectively as that of a diagram which is detailed in which it tells the story on its own just by seeing.

Nightingale's Rose Diagram: Florence Nightingale - who died over 100 years back - was a symbolic reformer and passionate campaigner for the health of soldiers during and after the Crimean war in 1854. During the war, much of the wounded British soldiers were transported across the Black Sea to Turkey. The condition of the Turkish hospitals in which the soldiers received treatment was particularly unpleasant. Nightingale, at the time, argued that the battlefield wounds of the soldiers could be eased and contained through measures such as appropriate nutrition, sanitation and physical exercise.

To do this, she cleverly adopted the idea of a pie chart to overlay rich and important information presented in a visually appealing manner telling an undeniable story. Figure 2.3 shows a re-creation of Nightingale's Rose Diagram. The entire circular element comprises of data for 12 months showing the mortality in hospitals, where the size of the "petals" show the number of soldiers falling ill.

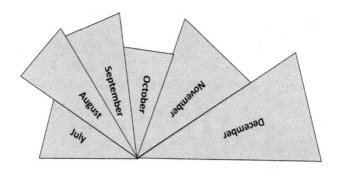

Figure 2.3: A representative visualization of Nightingale's Rose Diagram showing the rate at which soldiers were falling ill during the Crimean war in 1854.

SARS vs COVID-19: SARS (Severe Acute Respiratory Syndrome) is a virus induced epidemic that has affected people from worldwide in 2003. This virus first reported in Guangdong province of southern China - thought to have jumped from an animal, possibly bats or civet cats from a wet market in china, to humans. Similarly, the COVID-19 coronavirus pandemic is thought to have started in a wet market in the Hubei province in China. Both the epidemics are very similar in that they both are virus related with no known cures. However, the rate of infection between SARS and COVID-19 are very different. While the rate of infection for SARS was from 160 to 5000 cases in about 35 days, for COVID-19, this figure was from 120 to 5000 cases in about 10 days. In order to understand the high rate of infection of COVID-19, when compared to SARS, it would be useful to show both these rates on a chart, as shown in Figure 2.4. This would clearly highlight the difference in the rates of spread and clearly narrate the underlying story.

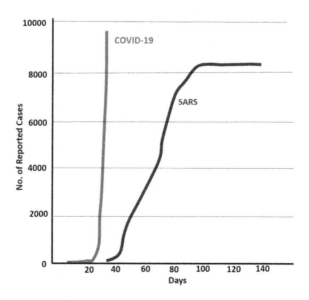

Figure 2.4: Comparison of the rate of infection between SARS and COVID-19.

Mapping the Mind

Data is often very unstructured. For the most part, handing such unstructured data is a daunting task for us. It is difficult for us to see the potential connections and make meaningful conclusions from such data. Effective visualization methods are the solution to this, giving a clean and easy way to interpret representations of data and conclusions made by analysis, showing clear connections and links that may have been hidden in rows upon rows of messy and potentially noisy data.

Thus, when trying to visualize complex datasets, it seems common sense indeed to use visualizations that humans are used to displaying the findings in the form of graphs or charts that is pleasing to the eye whilst still being informative.

Mind maps are one of these options, and in the realm of data visualization, mind maps are a recognized technique for all the stages in the process by data scientists. They promote structured thinking in a situation potentially involving large amounts of unstructured data that can be overwhelming, allowing for links to be made between subdivisions of the data even before processing that can then be carried over into a final visualization. Giving data this structure allows for easier comprehension and presentation, splitting into structured branches.

As well as the above, for a data scientist who is likely to be knowledgeable on topics such as treemaps within computer science, the structure is even more recognizable and has the potential to help to feed the data into algorithms involved in data mining and analyzing data that will then be visualized.

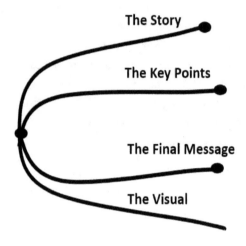

Figure 2.5: An example of a mind map that can be utilized for the process of constructing a good visualization.

Mind maps were popularized by British author Tony Buzan beginning in the late 1960s, though the concept of mapping long predates the idea. His findings were, after all, based on the centuries-old technique of the "concept mapping," utilized by people such as Leonardo Da Vinci. This hierarchical method of expanding ideas is useful for deliberating and refining different subtopics of a main idea or domain and allowing for use in almost - if not all - fields of research, and ranging from trivial to complex subjects.

In fact, they are so widely used in educational curriculums

that it is unlikely that many people - especially people handling data - would not have used a mind map at least once before. This suggests that the data presented in this way is something that almost anyone can interpret or create.

A well-documented example of information mapping that is not explicitly a mind map but follows similar ideas of mapping complex data is Beck's Tube map of the London Underground. Anyone who has used the London Underground will know fairly well that the station information on the Tube map is laid out in a consistent manner which barely resembles the physical layout of the network of stations beneath the ground. Although considered "radical" at first, it is clear to see that the simple mapping is easy to comprehend for people - hence why it took off as such a popular tool from the very beginning.

Anyone familiar with mind mapping can likely see the visual similarities between a map and a mind map structure as shown in Figure 2.5, and the similarities that extend to the core principle of being easy to process for humans, making sense of data that is otherwise confusing, in a simpler format.

There are a number of general strengths of the mind map techniques that also make them a good fit for good data visualization. As mentioned above, the main goal of data visualization is making the outcomes, connections, and large amounts of information visually appealing and understandable, which is something mind maps do exceptionally well. At any stage of the data analysis cycle, mind maps excel at visualizing complex data. This is seen as a bonus for data scientists trying to make sense of complex data they are analyzing.

Another strength that has been briefly touched on is the fact that almost everyone has likely had at least one encounter with mind maps in their life, meaning they are universally recognized and likely to be reliable as they are being used extensively with positive results.

Of course, where there are strengths to using these techniques, there are also pitfalls. One weakness of using mind maps for data visualization tasks is relevant to data scientists, especially, that mind maps do not allow for much detail to be presented on a small scale. Linked to this is the possibility for mind maps to become very large and in turn, overwhelming and counterproductive if a lot of detail or information is being fed into it.

Another weakness is the simple fact that not everyone is going to be a fan of mind maps - people may just not like them visually or find them unhelpful especially if they are partial to some other visualization techniques.

One main factor that must be taken into account is the opinions of people in the field who have experienced using mind maps, be it experts or everyday practitioners. If the general opinion is positive, it would suggest that the technique is fit for purpose. The result then would be pleasant user experience. Research on the use of mind maps suggests that a large proportion of people who have used mind maps consider it to be a useful tool.

Colors Complement Data Visualization

When we want to show data in diagrams, we need to apply colors. Sometimes colors are used for showing shapes while sometimes they are used for categorizing. Applying colors in our diagrams and charts can help readers to discover the values and trends faster. With the appropriate use of colors, we can create a graph or a chart that can tell a compelling story, and that can convey a message more effectively.

Choosing effective colors for each of the data elements in a visualization task for providing good discrimination is not a trivial task. Colors can convey emotions effectively and provide an appropriate impact on data visualization.

Modern color theory for data visualization has been built upon the work of scientists as well as artists. Many artists had many limitations in using color and material before the 16th century. Jan Van Eyck demonstrated how to use oil in color for painting. This kind of colors helped the artists to improve their painting to bring them close to reality. In 1704, Sir Isaac Newton proposed a color circle or color wheel named as Opticks which was based on rainbow colors in the natural light separated by prisms. In 1810, Geothe published the theory of colors, which demonstrated how humans understand colors without any physics and optical concepts. In the 1900s, Van Gogh and Fauvism Movement artists became famous for their color exploration. Then Josef Albers and Johannes Itten worked on color theory based on Van Gogh's initial work. In 1961, Itten published his work on the contrast of color, which is known "The Art of Color: The Subjective Experience and Objective Rational of color". Thus, Itten's color theory is an important tool for creating a good color scale.

Research shows that good visualization can be easy to understand, and many forms of information can be effectively conveyed with the use of an effective selection of colors. Color choice in visualization has been an interesting topic for many researchers, as they try to demonstrate various ways of choosing color scales. This task is similar to designing a book cover or a web page, and one needs to choose a good color set to optimize the final visual.

If colors are selected and utilized well, it can enhance and clarify the information presented in a chart. On the other hand, if colors are not applied carefully, it can confuse the audience. When we want to use colors, we should know which kind of information we want to show, and an important question one must ask is whether it is useful at all to use colors in the first place.

When it comes to choosing the colors in the visualization, there are some important concepts one must bear in mind. For example, color contrast and analogy is an important factor to draw attention to. In addition, color has three dimensions: hue, value, chroma. Hue is identified with names of the color, e.g., yellow or red. Value defines the lightness of the color and chroma explains an object's colorfulness, i.e., an object with a high chroma is vivid and with low chroma is grayish.

In order to obtain the best results in color selection, it is appropriate to limit the level of hue used in the visualization. For this reason, there are three schemas for picking colors for effective data visualization. They are,

- multi-hue palettes,
- single-hue scale,
- and divergent (two-hue) scales.

When we want to make different categories, we can use a multi-hue schema, e.g., in a pie chart or on a map. These types of methods are not based on a single value. There are some notable points, such as the visual equidistance and the hue range that we should pay attention to. For example, to show one numerical variable in different areas, we can use the single-hue method. Also, we can use divergent scales for presenting transition from a to b or c.

Any given dataset essentially can be divided into three categories. They are qualitative, continuous, dissimilar. A qualitative dataset can be visualized using very distinguishable colors. A dissimilar dataset can be visualized with varying surrounding colors with a very neutral color in the center. A continuous dataset can be visualized using a color pallet with varying uniformity in lightness and saturation.

As mentioned, for choosing colors in visualization, there are some important aspects one should consider. These include color limitation, the emotion of the chosen colors and the type of design of the color palette chosen.

Colors play an important role in conveying human emotions and in conveying crucial stories. This may in part be hard-wired, or it may be cultural. For example, red is often associated with danger, power, and is a sign of warning. On the other hand, the color blue - which is the color of the sea and the sky - is often associated with calmness, serenity and a sense of professionalism.

Often a combination of one or two colors can be used to convey an effective message in data visualization. For example, putting up the most important message in your graph using a stronger color helps to highlight it more. A title or a part of the line graph drawn in red can be striking and will stick out more. The use of colored heat maps, in fact, act as a great aid in data visualization.

Thus, in compelling visualizations, the use of colors helps the user to receive an effective message, it can provide an emotional engagement with the audience, and it can help capture the user's attention selectively.

Glyphs for Data Visualization

Glyphs are one of the most common pattern selection tools for visual design. Glyphs are a collection of small visual objects which are used to conceal various attribute dimensions of an input data space. In other words, a glyph can be a small visual object that gives information of a data record, also can individually put in display space and finally, glyphs are visual signs but are different from icons and symbols (Borgo et al. 2013)

Glyphs and their practical use have been known to man many years before the development of data visualization. Those who first came across the idea were the ancient Greeks. Although from the Paleolithic age, glyphs are used widely as cave paintings and from the Neolithic age glyphs are the first forms of the communication system. It is actually very interesting that around the world these first forms of communication systems are very similar. The first logographic writing system developed from the Chinese is based in the hieroglyphics. The Egyptians developed their own writing system based in logographic, alphabetic, and ideographic elements.

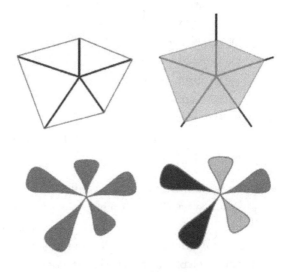

Figure 2.6: Examples of glyphs where the number of arms in the star pattern show the number of variables and the length and the variation in the width of the arms represents the numerical variations in the variables.

In order to understand more, the importance of glyph based techniques in the field of data visualization, we need to examine topics where glyphs were part of the solution. In big data science, data analysts often have to deal with large and more complex datasets. This is also known as solving the problem of clustering in data science. The solution to this problem is to find a proper visualization technique that lets the user do different types of analysis on a dataset. For this sort of problem, the use of a glyph based solutions appears to be very appropriate.

Glyphs are a popular method for conveying information visually. Each variable for a given data is mapped onto an attribute of a specific shape or symbol and constructed in a 2D or 3D visualization space. A glyph is a small visual object, which can be used independently and constructively to represent an attribute of a data record. Each glyph can be placed spatially and independently from others, while sometimes they can be spatially connected. Glyphs can make use of visual features of other types of signs such as icons, indices and symbols.

It is not always easy to design a glyph-based visualization, although it was a widespread opinion for a long time that knowing the basic principles of it will be enough to use it successfully. Glyph based visualization has three major characteristics: glyph shape: basic or composite, glyph appearance: color, transparency, texture and glyph placement in the display. For both (basic or composite) glyph shapes and the glyph appearance, a continuous mapping or a discrete mapping can be used to communicate information based on the glyph's properties.

Glyph Shape is the key property, and it is essential that it is observable easily and clearly. The glyph shapes are primarily used to convey information because the observation of shapes is more accurate than the perception of quantities represented by colors. There are two main groups of glyph shapes: a) Basic - the geometric objects that can be adjusted by changing their geometric properties and b) Composite -

the composed of the basic glyph shapes. It often requires specialized mapping functions - more than basic glyph shapes - and it is often used to display multidimensional data, where each attribute can be connected with an attribute of the data.

Glyph Appearance is the property most commonly used to convey information. For example, a combination of color, transparency and texture form a typical glyph appearance. It is difficult to achieve an absolute quantification using a continuous color mapping because variances in color are more difficult to recognize than, for instance, spatial distances. A color scale is preferable when it varies in hue and luminance. Employing the transparency in the color coding is a common extension, but it makes the perception of occlusion relations harder, so using it is expected to hamper the visual perception of objects. Textures can be used, for instance, to convey directional information which helps to communicate more complex information through the glyph appearance.

Glyph Placement is very important to achieve a beneficial glyph based visualization. Glyph placement can be based either on the regular grid or on the location of the attributes of the dataset under consideration. There are basic considerations for placing the glyphs. They include,

- selecting a placement strategy, whether it is data-driven or structure-driven,
- deciding whether the overlapping between glyphs is allowed or not, which can have a significant effect on the size of the dataset that can be depicted,

- knowing the trade-off between optimized screen utilization,
- and knowing whether the glyph positions can be adjusted after the initial placement for improving visibility at the cost of distorting the computed position.

Glyphs are typically small and designed with high similarity to achieve many concepts such as mapping consistency, learning and memorization. They are restricted in terms of how accurately they can convey data due to their size and the limits of our visual perception system, because of that they are vulnerable to many perceptual errors which could lead to difficulties in glyph differentiation.

In visualization, screen space and resolution are often limited. As a result, placing a few glyphs can lead to missing contextual information, and on the other hand, placing too many glyphs over the entire space can introduce severe visual occlusion. Hence, occlusion is a key challenge in generating effective glyphs based visualization. As a result, when just a few data attributes need to be visualized, glyph based visualizations can be most effective.

Thus, the number of data records that can be visualized effectively with glyphs could also be limited. Representing a big dataset through glyphs can result in insignificant occlusion. Reducing the size of the glyphs is one of the solutions, which could make the detection of patterns more difficult. Therefore, in general, glyphs are mainly appropriate for qualitative analysis of datasets of modest size.

Chernoff's Faces: An example to highlight the use of glyphs in data visualization is Chernoff's faces. Chernoff's faces were introduced into the field of data visualization by Herman Chertoff in 1973. This method is most commonly used to exhibit data in a convenient form, to assist the viewer in exploring clusters, outliers, and fluctuations with time. Chernoff faces can represent multivariate data and show their complex relationships. It is a mechanism to provide a bird's eye view to the data and provide indications for applying more appropriate statistical analysis. Chernoff's faces are made up of two-dimensional line drawings with human facial features. An example of Chernoff's faces is shown below in Figure 2.7.

Figure 2.7: Examples of Chernoff's faces, whereby the variables in the dataset correspond to the parts of the face. The emotional changes in the selected parts of the face show the variation in the numerical values of the chosen variables.

When working with a multidimensional dataset, certain facial features and characteristics such as eyes, ears, nose, and mouth can be mapped to variables. It is widely acknowledged that human beings are proficient at recognizing faces and can observe minor changes in facial characteristics. This is the main reasoning of the application of Chernoff's faces in visualizing and examining data.

Just like all other various techniques used to study multidimensional data have their own advantages and disadvantages, Chernoff's faces has several distinct strengths over other representational techniques. Along with the strengths, there are also weaknesses in this method.

The greatest strength of this method is the fact that human faces are easily recognized and described. As humans, we are naturally good at studying faces and learning to differentiate distinct facial characteristics. Compared to metroglyphes and other forms of data visualization, variations in human faces are far easier to detect. Furthermore, examining faces means that we can rely on a commonality of a language, i.e., when we tend to speak about certain properties of the human face, such as the length of the nose or the width of the mouth, there is less room for confusion.

Another advantage of using Chernoff's faces is that the viewer can link facial characteristics with the physical meaning of each variable. For example, the smile can be used to represent either as a pass or fail variable. The eyes may indicate the scale of emotion. The height of the forehead can determine intelligence.

Contrary to the benefits mentioned above of Chernoff's

faces, this technique also shares major drawbacks. The most obvious weakness that can be discussed is that a plotting device might be required to draw a standard Chernoff face. Similarly, a crucial weakness with the Chernoff's faces is that the built-in dependencies of the facial features may misrepresent the data visualization enough to cause erroneous impressions. In addition, there are severe challenges that may arise when viewing the faces, as the number of variables to be represented increases. If the faces being examined are alike, this case will be particularly true. However, if there are two or three unique variables, there will not be a lot of obstacles.

The Chernoff's faces is a popular graphical entity which can be used to illustrate and study multidimensional data. When properly employed, it gives beneficial information into the nature of data and has significant benefits over the other forms of graphical techniques. The main criticism of this method is its partiality. However, this can be considered as a constructive feature rather than a weakness. Furthermore, it can be argued that the problem of facial feature dependencies can be solved. From the research conducted, it is evident that there have been many interesting applications of Chernoff's faces – including cluster analysis, outlier detection methods, distributional studies, and time-series analysis. Despite its several weaknesses, the Chernoff's faces concept is seen as an effective tool for tasks involving multivariate data analysis.

Gestalt Principles

Any large problem can be solved by constructively dividing into a sum of smaller problems, each of which may have a feasible solution. If one considers how the human visual system sees, objects or scenarios, one can say there exist a set of consentient elements that helps us to obtain meaningful conclusions from them. These essential mechanisms by which the brain sees information is through, proximity, similarity, continuity, closure, connection, and enclosure which are identified as the Gestalt (meaning unified) principles (Todorovic, 2008).

Proximity: The closer the certain types of visuals are, the more we feel that they are somehow related. If we want to emphasize the close connection between two or many types of variables in a dataset, we could cluster them together, either in the form of glyphs or colors. This would provide the impression of groups and closer relationships for the chosen elements in the dataset.

Similarity: Colors or objects which are similar will convey the impression that they belong to the same class or group. For example, one could use the color red to indicate the level of loss and the color green to represent the level of profit in various businesses. The red and green, in this case, can be represented in the form of lines or other objects and may reside in separate locations of the visualization. However, the visual relation with the same color will be sufficient to show the similarities.

Enclosure: In order to show that a number of variables in a dataset belong to the same category of classification, it may be helpful to put them into groups with some of the marked borders or enclose. Such enclosures provide the user with the impression that the variables are distinct and related in some way. It is important to note that the level of emphasis on the border or the enclosure, i.e. the strength of the color or line thickness will further enhance the level of distinctness of the chosen the variable or objects in the dataset.

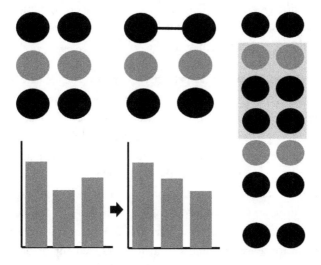

Figure 2.8: Examples from the Gestalt principles – proximity, similarity, enclosure and closure are important elements to consider when constructing meaningful visualizations.

Closure: As much as it sounds implausible, an incomplete structure or entity is seen to be closed by our eyes. A good example is the Cartesian lines we draw to represent the entire (infinite) two-dimensional space. Two short pieces of lines perpendicular to each other (one horizontal and one vertical) is sufficient for us to imagine the entire two-dimensional space in which data is often presented. Thus, the principle of closure asserts that open structures are perceived to be closed, full and integrated.

Prägnanz: In essence, Prägnanz is the central element of the Gestalt law. The word Prägnanz comes from German meaning "pithiness" which roughly to translates to being succinctly concise. The human brain hates complexity. Conversely, we love simplicity. We love patterns that are ordered, regular, even and alike.

The Gestalt principles effectively try to encapsulate this human mind's viewpoint to make sense and to organize visual scenes. It is important, whenever possible, to arrange the visualization in some form of logical order. Characteristics such as color, size and shape may be used in similar forms to highlight the relationship between groups. For an effective visualization, it would be important to identify and create groupings which are arranged and supported by proximity. It would also be useful to utilize commonsense and linearity in the arrangement of objects within the visualization to show the relationships and remove the burden of visual obscurity.

Elements of Effective Visualization

The prime aim of any visualization must be to find a suitable medium to filter through large amounts of data to extract knowledge from it and present it to the audience with a compelling narrative. Any successful visualization must be constructed with key some elements in mind. The following are the essential elements one must adopt in constructing successful visualization.

The Audience: One of the most important pieces of exercises one must do for creating an effective visualization is to know the audience to which it is presented. Knowing the audience is understanding to tailor and inspire the contents and present the visualization in an engaging manner. It is important to establish the aims of the visualization and how these aims may be seen from the point of view of the audience. While some audiences may require extensive technical details hidden in the data, others may be interested in just the headlines. Being able to know in advance the level of detail, the technical know-how of the audience and the level of engagement required will not only help to construct an effective data visualization but also help to narrate the main points one wants to convey.

The Story: The chance of conveying an important message to a target audience is higher if the message is encapsulated in a well-formulated story. A good story will have a clear beginning, engaging middle and final important message. The story should highlight important elements the visualization must convey, including any comparisons as well as similarities that you may want to draw the attention of the audience. It is, therefore, important to understand the audience, the problem at hand and formulate a narrative which is accurate and appealing to the visualizer. The impact of your data in terms of trends, peaks and troughs should also be highlighted. This is particularly important in today's digitally savvy fast-paced world where data is coming to us in an explosive fashion and therefore extracting as well as presenting knowledge from data should be made as appealing as possible.

The Chart: The technique or the method of visualization has always to match with the dataset, the audience and the messages to be conveyed. The chart chosen does not have to be often complex. For example, for a lay audience, simple bar graphs or pie charts may often be the best chart form to put forward the desired message in a visual form. There are four key presentation needs for any visualization. They are comparison, composition, distribution and relationship. Accordingly, depending on the need of the visualization, the most appropriate chart should be chosen. The choice of the chart should also depend on the number of variables to be displayed, the amount of data, and whether the data is time-dependent or not.

The Layout: The use of hierarchy, ordering and the proper use of color are very important to convey the desired message. With the right choice of a suitable layout, it is important to keep the visualization as simple as possible so the audience can be drawn into the important elements of the visualization with minimal cognitive effort. Consistent use of color, hues and chroma will help to enhance the visualization and provide a notable impact. Data to be visualized often comes in complex and unstructured forms. It becomes important to choose the data in a logical and organized manner in order to ensure the correct data forms are being used to analyse and reach a correct decision through the chosen visualization.

Discussions

Back in ancient times, humans have used different symbols and signs to convey different information or messages. It has been known that around the 2nd-century CE, people have started to use tables for ordering different data and information. However, these visualizations were not quantitative measurements until the 17th century when the French philosopher and mathematician Rene Descartes invented the two-dimensional coordinate system. After Descartes, the Scotsman William Playfair was first to use the two-dimensional system for graphical representation and quantitative measurements. Also, he discovered the bar graphs and pie charts.

Human perception and data visualization are two related processes which cannot be thought to unrelated. The human brain can accept and understand images way much easier and faster than reading or listening. Therefore, visualization was an old technique that humans used to convey different messages and information in the first place. Visualization models were further expanded and developed with the increase of data and the advent of technology. Compared to rapid developments in technology, human perception has not changed drastically over the years. Thus, the process of visualization has not radically changed. Nonetheless, technology has helped with our sense of visualization through rich forms of graphics and advanced software for the representation of data digitally.

Nowadays, there are many ways to represent and visualize data, but it is always important to evaluate the quality of visual representations based on human perception. To further improve the accuracy and effectiveness of data visualization, further studies in human cognition and psychology should be conducted. In this way, data visualization would further contribute to better data patterns and analytics.

There are various ways one may find effective stories to tell from data. Finding trends, correlations or outliers in the data would be a good starting point of an effective story. For example, if you are able to find a consistent pattern in the dataset where you could identify the growth in crimes in cities around the world that will be a trend to report in the form of a visualization. If you can find the number of drug-related gangs and crime in cities that will be a potential correlation to report to. If you can find a sudden growth of criminal activity in a certain city that will be an outlier which can be visualized among other the crime rates of other cities which will tell an effective story.

In general, when it comes to human perceptions of data visualization, elements such as shape and space should be considered as well. Gestalt's theory claims that selecting a good shape is an important factor for the human brain to process the information taken through visual images. Furthermore, distances between points, size of the overlapping of objects, texture gradient, light and shade are important elements for visual data representation.

One of the best visual design practices is to support comprehension by keeping it simple, avoiding noise in the visual display. This includes removing extraneous gridlines, avoiding color gradation or anything that does not support the encoding of the information from the data, to make it easy for the viewer to interoperate and identify the patterns in data

After simplification, emphasis can be applied to help the audience in encoding and understanding the information.

Utilizing attention-guiding style components, like orientation and distinction, significantly improve the precision of interpretation and long term information memory.

In constructing an effective visualization, one must look for opportunities to enhance all your communication, whether internal or external, with data visualization. One must start with a good question, then look for the data that can help answer or provide more insight into the problem. Working with a solid dataset that includes relevant data from a reputable source is an important part of data visualization. Crafting a cohesive narrative around your key data points and following best practices in data visualization will ensure the information presented gives a clear message with maximum possible impact.

References

M. Friendly, "Visions and Re-visions of Charles Joseph Minard", Journal of Educational and Behavioral Statistics, 27(1), 31-51, (2002).

L. Brasseur, "Florence Nightingale's Visual Rhetoric in the Rose Diagrams", Technical Communication Quarterly, 14(2), 161-182, (2005).

D. Todorovic, "Gestalt principles", Scholarpedia, 3(12): 5345, (2008).

R. Borgo, J. Kehrer, D. H. S. Chung, E. Maguire, R.S. Laramee, H. Hauser, M. Ward, and M. Chen, M. "Glyph-based Visualization: Foundations, Design Guidelines, Techniques and Applications", Eurographics State of the Art Reports, 39-63, (2013).

4

ESSENTIAL METHODS AND TECHNIQUES FOR DATA VISUALIZATION

In the present day, data is created constantly from very many sources, for example, through sensor devices and social media, and it is growing at an unprecedented rate in different forms in volume, velocity and variety. Many challenges are being faced on how to handle, analyze and make sense of such huge data in order to turn them into useful information and knowledge.

Data visualization is an integral part of the process of understanding data as it helps to present extracted knowledge to users in an understandable form. In addition, visualization diagrams such as histograms, scatter plots and networks are used for the visual inspection of datasets to identify outliers or display data summaries and distributions.

Selecting a technique for converting our numerical data into graphical representation depends on the type of the data (e.g. nominal, ordinal, quantitative), dimensions of attributes (e.g. univariate, bivariate, multivariate), data structures (e.g. 1D/Linear, 2D/Planar, 3D/Volumetric, multi-dimensional data, hierarchical, networks) and also the level of understanding of available techniques to the user.

Data analysts may use a variety of techniques to give shape

to data. The choice of the technique is not random, and scientists must be cautious because not only the user has to understand what is present in the data but also the meaning of the results. All these can affect the final output if inappropriate techniques are used.

The prime goal of choosing the right method for visualization is to communicate effectively to a selected audience, answering a question for which the solution has objectivity and provides some form of insight. Thus, when choosing a suitable method of visualization, the audience to which the message is communicated and the purpose of the visual communication need proper identification.

Audience: The data to be visualized has to be always considered carefully by bearing in mind the target audience. If your target audience is an everyday consumer, then a simple visualization such as a pie chart or a column chart representing the variation of quantities may be the right approach. Conversely, if you are communicating a message to an experienced researcher or a technically knowledgeable decision-maker, then your visualization may contain matrix plots or networks.

Purpose: Depending on the reason we would like to create a visualization from the data we may have, different forms of visualization may be invoked. In order to emphasize individual narratives, it may be useful to choose the right type of graph, shape and color combinations. To show the relationship between two quantities, one may choose a simple scatter plot whereas to show the broad difference between two quantities, and one could choose a bubble chart with varying sizes or contrasting colors.

In the world of data visualization, there exist a rich variety of methods and techniques. It will be an extremely tedious job to list all these methods and techniques. However, for someone interested in being immersed in the world of data visualization, it is crucial to have in-depth knowledge of the most common methods and techniques used in data visualization. Types of commonly used methods and techniques can be broadly divided into, charts, histograms, maps and diagrams.

Charts

One of the easiest ways to show the variation of values in a dataset containing a small number of variables is the use of charts. Common chart types include column charts, line charts and pie charts. Figure 4.1 shows examples of common chart types.

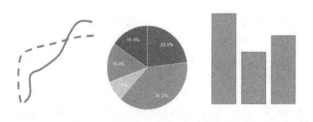

Figure 4.1: Examples of common chart types used in data visualization – line graph, pie chart and bar graph.

Column Chart: The column chart is one of the most common visualization techniques. Column charts are usually used to express datasets over time. While the data variables are generally presented along the horizontal axis, the measured values for those variables considered are displayed vertically. Though color variations can be utilized on the bars across the charts, the use of color is often kept minimal and consistent. Column charts are easy to read and understand. However, with too many variables, the chart can be cluttered and confusing to interpret.

Line Chart: A line graph is one of the easiest and most common ways of visualizing the trends of values for a given number of variables. The trend can be progress or a change that usually occur over time. Line graphs are also useful when the data is somewhat continuous. Again, line chart visualizations can be useful when the number of variables considered is sufficiently small as the number of lines in the graph increases the harder it becomes to visualize and understand the graph.

Pie Chart: The pie chart is effectively the visualization of the various data variable in a dataset adding up to a whole entity. In essence, it shows each variable considered in its numerical proportion.

Bubble Chart: Bubble chart is a common data visualization tool to show three or more dimensional data on a flat, 2D graph. By using this tool, entities are plotted in such a way that the x and y axes represent the first two variables and bubbles of varying size represent values of the third variable. Limited information can be added on the fourth variable by assigning colors to the bubbles. Along with mapping and rank order, bubble charts provide ways to organize complex information, discover insights and stimulate discussions. Bubble plots also can offer some systematic directions for setting up priorities and making decisions. Figure 4.2 shows an outline of a typical bubble chart.

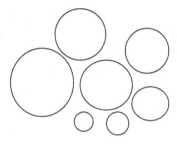

Figure 4.2: An outline of a bubble chart – the number of bubbles may represent the variables in the dataset while their sizes represent the numerical value associated with the variables.

Bubble charts can be successfully utilized to analyze data from social, medical, economic, and many other disciplines to find patterns and correlations. For instance, it can be used to show that increasing prices of cigarettes prevent people from smoking and decrease the cases of lung cancer per capita.

Thus, bubble charts are useful visualization tools to analyze and uncover underlying patterns and correlations. Bubble charts are meaningful when visualizing a dataset of three or four variables, mainly because the graphical representation of the segmentation provided by bubble charts enable us to visualize the clusters and obtain information about patterns and correlations between variables. Hence, the bubble chart is one of the simplest and easy visualization tools that convey underlying insights about data and offer significant directions to set up priorities and make decisions.

However, despite having a number of advantages, bubble charts also have a number of drawbacks. For example, bubble charts are only good at dealing with smaller datasets. As with extensive data, too many bubbles on the chart can make it harder to read. Further, with proportional area charts, if the size of the circle is not drawn according to the area of the circles, it can lead to change the size of circle exponentially and lead to misinterpretations of the chart. Similarly, often smaller bubbles are hard to see, if they are covered by the larger sized bubbles. Moreover, the bubble chart is most useful if the data has only positive values.

The bubble chart is a powerful visualization tool, yet it requires to be used on the right datasets with at least three variables. Some background information must be added with the chart as the bubble charts are unable to explain "why" and "how" type of questions. The use of a transparent color for the bubbles often helps to see the smaller bubbles covered behind the larger ones.

Figure 4.3: An example of a scatter graph with a correlation line showing the commonality of the variation between the two variables considered.

Scatter Plot: A scatter plot is usually used to display the variation between two variables in a given dataset to show the distributions. A common reason for using a scatter plot for visualization is for the identification of any existing correlation between the variables. In this sense, a scatter plot can show patterns and gaps in the dataset. A scatter plot may well be used to identify the correlation between the two variable though a point of worthy of noting here is that correlation does not necessarily mean causation, i.e. simply because if there is a relationship between the two variables, it does not mean that changes in one variable are responsible for the corresponding change in the other variable. Figure 4.3 shows a typical scatter plot where the correlation line shows the commonality of the variation between the two variables considered.

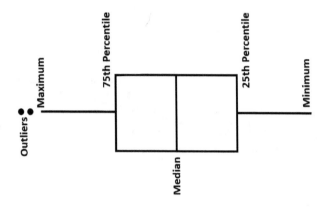

Figure 4.4: An example of a box plot. A box plot shows the minimum, maximum, median and the common percentiles as well as the outliers in the dataset.

Boxplot: Boxplot visualization can show the distribution in a dataset into retrospective quartiles. A boxplot shows the minimum and maximum values in the dataset, the first quartile (25th percentile), the median, the third quartile (75th percentile) and any outliers in the dataset as shown in Figure 4.4.

Histograms

Histogram plots are one of the most well-known and efficient visualization tools that can provide essential information regarding the underlying frequency distribution, and skewness of data, in the form of bar graphs. Since long, histogram plots have been applied as visual aids in many areas. However, in the last few decades, they have gained significant success in database applications where they have been utilized efficiently to compress and approximate large data distributions. Besides this, they are also of greater importance in computer vision and image processing.

Interestingly, histograms have long been used in the past even before they were specifically assigned with any name. The word "histogram" was introduced by a popular statistician, Karl Pearson, to refer to graphical presentations. However, the earliest forms of histograms were perceived as bar charts. In 1786, bar charts were mentioned for the first time in literature, in a book called "The Commercial and Political Atlas" written by William Playfair. In his reported work, the bar charts represented import and export between Scotland and seventeen other countries. Although Playfair was not confident about his invention, his concept of bar charts were being applied by many in the following years. For example, in 1859, Florence Nightingale used bar charts to compare the rates of mortality.

A histogram demonstrates the frequency distribution of continuous datasets through a bar graph. The x-axis in the graph denotes the class-intervals, i.e. the range of values into which the measurements can fall. Moreover, the bars in the histogram plot demonstrate two important parameters, i.e. width and height. In case of a histogram with class intervals of equal size, the height represents the frequency of values within an interval, and width represents the length of the class interval. At the same time, the y-axis is the scale representing the frequency. However, in case of a histogram with class intervals of varying size, the frequency is presented by the area of the bar instead of the height of the bar, and the y-axis represents frequency density instead of frequency.

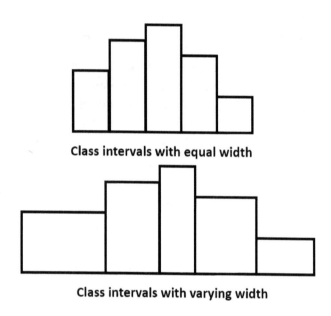

Class intervals with equal width

Class intervals with varying width

Figure 4.5: Histogram plots representing variation in the width.

In Figure 4.5, it is shown a histogram with equi-width histogram (intervals of equal size) in which the frequency of people falling ill in a particular range of age is represented through the height of the bar. Figure 4.5 also shows a histogram with class intervals of varying size. Note that in contrast to bar charts, histograms do not have gaps between class intervals. However, the absence of histogram indicates zero frequencies.

If we refer to the appropriate width size of the class intervals (bins) and the number of class intervals in a histogram, there is no 'best' size defined for both. However, it is recommended that the width of class intervals shall neither be very small nor very large. This concept can be better illustrated in Figure 4.6, which shows histograms of varying bin sizes.

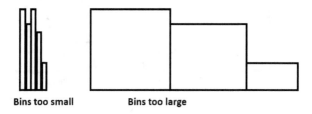

Bins too small   **Bins too large**

Figure 4.6: Histograms with varying bin sizes.

In comparison with the histogram represented in Figure 4.6, the left histogram displayed in Figure 4.6 shows that the width of the class intervals has been kept very small while the number of class intervals produced is high. Hence, a histogram with such features fails to represent the underlying pattern of frequency distribution clearly. In contrast, in the histogram in the right, the size of class intervals is significantly large, and the number of class intervals is too low to represent the underlying trend in the data. Based on this, it can be concluded that it is critical to choose the appropriate number, and width size, of class intervals for the effective representation of data through histograms.

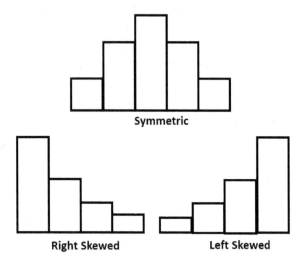

Symmetric

Right Skewed   **Left Skewed**

Figure 4.7: Example histograms showing symmetric, right and left skew in the data.

The histogram plot attains a bell shape when the data is normally distributed, which shows that the highest point is in the center with two symmetrical slopes around it on both sides. However, real data distributions are often not normal. They are rather skewed towards the right or left. If the curve is skewed towards the right, it is called a positively skewed curve, and otherwise, if skewed towards left, it is called a negatively skewed curve. Figure 4.7 illustrates the three kinds of distributions.

In databases, histograms have been successfully applied to compress and approximate data distributions so that they can be stored efficiently. The efficiency of histograms in dealing with big data distributions in databases is dependent on the techniques utilized for partitioning the data, approximating frequencies and values within each class interval. The partitioning of data is performed by taking into account parameters (which in most cases include frequency, attribute value and area) that can characterize data elements. Thus, the efficiency of the histogram in approximating data distributions for the design of histogram shall be made flexible with no defined frequencies for each interval. Instead, it should have a different optimal approximation approach for each class interval within a histogram. Moreover, histograms are utilized in image processing such that, provided an image and a pixel feature, for every single value of the feature, a histogram would attain the number of pixels having that value. A histogram, based on this strategy, summarizes the features of an image and can, therefore, be very beneficial in image compression and recognition of identical images.

Histograms are also meaningful in summarizing 'large' distributions of numeric datasets mainly because the measurements in the histogram are represented as class intervals - also called bins - not as single data points. Different shapes of the histogram plots convey significant information about the underlying distributions of data. This can have a higher impact on decision-making for problems defined through the data given.

It is noteworthy that histograms have been efficiently applied in databases to compress large data distributions which are difficult to be stored otherwise. Interestingly, a number of successful optimal histograms have been constructed using different partitioning constraints, frequency and value approximation techniques to produce the desired compression results. Likewise, histograms have also gained huge success in image processing. However, despite having a number of advantages, histograms suffer due to a few drawbacks. For example, it can only be applied to continuous data and fails to deal with any other data type. Further, choosing the appropriate number of class intervals and the right amount of information represented through each interval is a critical step in representing data through a histogram.

As mentioned above, the use of too many or too few class intervals can be misleading. Moreover, it is important to point out is that from a practical perspective, the histograms with class intervals of varying size are not commonly used. However, research suggests that varying size of class intervals in a histogram can be more effective in the sense that wider class intervals can be used to represent the regions with low density in order to lessen the noise caused due to sampling errors.

On the other hand, the higher density regions can be represented through narrower class intervals to produce higher precision to the approximation of density. Unfortunately, the practical implications of this concept cannot be found significant. Further, it is also interpreted that histograms cannot be considered useful for a comparative analysis between multiple categories as the comparison of different histograms may be misleading.

Thus, histogram plots demonstrate great effectiveness in displaying a graphical representation of large dataset distributions. The variations in shape provide the underlying patterns of distribution of data, which can be significant in problem investigation dealing with big data. Advanced applications of histograms in the areas of image processing and databases suggest that many problems relevant to big data distributions can be solved using histograms. However, to make histograms more useful, there is still research going on to find the appropriate balance between the number of class intervals and the amount of information contained in each class interval. Further, the potential of histograms to deal with distributions of different data types - other than continuous data - is a key question that needs to be addressed in future.

Maps and Diagrams

Maps and diagrams in data visualization allow the demonstration of the variations in the data in a matrix form. Common forms of maps and diagrams used in data visualizations are the tree maps, heat maps and hyperbolic trees. Figure 4.8 shows some examples of maps used in data visualization.

Treemaps: A treemap displays hierarchical data using a nested figure – usually in the form of rectangles. It has a tree structure whereby the size of the rectangle representing the specific branch in the tree structure. Treemaps are an efficient way of displaying a large number of variables and their variations.

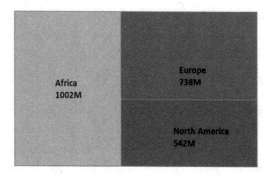

Figure 4.8: An example of a map used in data visualization.

Heat maps: A heat map represents the data graphically where the data are distributed in a matrix form represented using various colors. Heat maps are often used to obtain a general overview of the distributions in the data. Using a heat map one can therefore quickly get the general sense of the state and the impact of a large number of variables within a dataset.

Tools for Data Visualization

There are plenty of visualization tools out there, and it is difficult to list them and describe their individual functionality since such a list would be quite exhaustive. However, here are some of the common tools available for plotting visualization.

• Essential tools - Among the Microsoft Office suite, Word, Excel and PowerPoint all have simple data processing and visualization functionality. Due to the worldwide popularity of the Windows system, they were once the number one choice for people to process data. Of course, packages such as Word Excel and PowerPoint cannot handle large data. However, for individual users and small business owners, the ease of availability and the simple and straightforward user interface allows them to be used for most of their data visualization tasks.

• Tableau – is widely used for data science and business intelligence. It can be used to visualize data interactively and showcase insights.

• Qlikview - is a visualization based reporting tool. It can create a wide variety of dashboards for analysts and decision-makers.

• Sisense – is widely used for business intelligence. It can analyze and visualize multiple and complex big datasets.

• Plotly - is a high-level charting library with over 30 types of charts.

• Fusioncharts - is one of the most comprehensive charting libraries with over 100 chart type and over 200 map types. Being a JavaScript based tool, it is particularly suitable for interactive web based applications.

• Power BI – is a professional data analytics and visualization tool that can bring together separate datasets into clear visual forms.

• Gephi – is an interactive tool that can help visualize complex systems and dynamics. It is particularly useful for producing hierarchical graphs.

• NodeXL - is an intuitive visualization tool. It is particularly good for graphing and visualization of complex networks.

• Matlab - is a programming environment with a powerful visualization tool. Matlab is particularly suited for scientific and mathematical visualizations.

• Mathematica - is a flexible tool for charting and information visualization.

• Maple - is a modelling and simulation software package with built-in visualization tools for extensive plotting functionalities.

• R - has a versatile visualization tool with inbuilt functions and libraries for extensive data analysis and visual presentations.

Above, we have highlighted some of the most common software tools available for data visualization. Depending on the circumstances and individual needs, some tools could be more suitable than the others for a particular task. For example, for educational or scientific purposes software like Matlab, Mathematica, Maple, and R may prove to be the best options. Furthermore, for tasks like reporting and business intelligence (which is of commercial concern), tools like Tableau, Plotly and Power BI are the preferred choices because of their simple and friendly design and interface. Such tools often assume the user has no computer programming background.

At the beginner level software like Excel, PowerPoint, or Raw Graphs are more suitable for individuals who require to produce quick visualization with smaller datasets. On the other hand, professional level software like Tableau is expensive and requires training before use. Of course, this kind of software also offers more sophisticated capabilities for processing and visualizing big data. Hence, this kind of data visualization software is more suited for larger companies and organizations. Similarly, visualization tools with programming tools – such as Matlab and Mathematica often require some degree of programming and therefore are more suited for domain experts, data engineers and data scientists. And, such tools can integrate data mining, data analysis and data visualization to produce powerful data analytics solutions.

An Example

At the bank ABC recently, they have identified a problem in which many of its customers have been leaving the bank. It has been identified that the customers are leaving at a higher rate, unlike the common churn rate that has been recorded in the banking industry. The bank needs to investigate the situation to find out what is exactly happening with their customers, and they need insight into this problem so that they can come up with ways to fix it.

Therefore, the bank took a sample data from their customer database containing 10,000 records. They were interested in answering questions such as why the customers are leaving the bank and what are the similarities between the customers who left and those who are still active, what types of customers are leaving, which branches or countries are affected the most, and furthermore, they wanted to predict if a customer will leave or not.

In order to address these questions, the first step is to carry out some exploratory data analysis using the data available and discover any anomalies there may be. Since the interest is to predict customer behavior, based on the observed dataset, these types of problems are known as classification problems.

Classification is the problem of identifying which set of categories a new observation belongs to, for example, whether the customer will leave the bank or not. For example, a technique known as logistic regression allows us to solve classification problems, whereby we try to predict discrete categories to which the answers to the questions raised can be classified. A standard convention for data classification is to use a binary classifier, i.e. to have two classes 0 and 1, for say leave or stay.

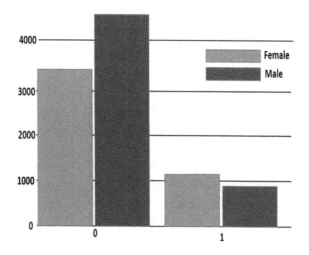

Figure 4.9: A count plot can be effectively used to show the churn across gender.

A count plot – as shown in Figure 4.9 - can be utilized to show the churn rates based on gender where 0 means stay, and 1 means leave. From the graph, it can be noted that female customers are most likely to leave the bank because they have the highest churn rate in contrast to male customers.

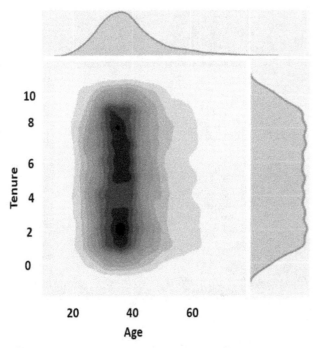

Figure 4.10: A joint plot showing how the ages of the customers are related to the tenure of banking.

Figure 4.10 shows a joint plot showing the distribution of customer by age (in the *x*-axis) versus tenure (in the *y*-axis). From this plot, we can infer that customers between ages 25 and 45 years stay longer with the bank.

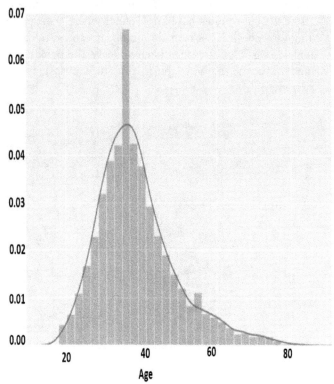

Figure 4.11: A univariate distribution plot showing the distribution of customers by age.

Figure 4.11 is a plot showing a univariate distribution of customers by age. It can be inferred from the plot that the majority of the customers of the bank are in the age group of 30 to 45 years.

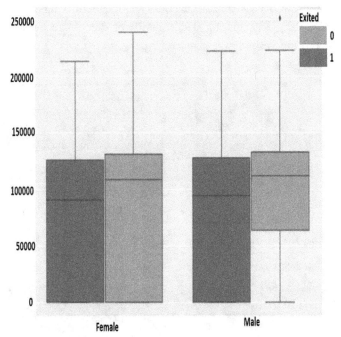

Figure 4.12: A box plot showing the distribution of bank balance across gender.

Figure 4.12 is a boxplot showing the distribution of the bank balance based on gender. The line in the middle of the box represents the median, the bottom line represents the first quartile, the top line represents the second quartile, the straight line is the whisker, and the dot represents an outlier.

The first method used in this example is for the visual exploration of the raw data. This method of analysis plays a crucial role in any model development for a final visualization. It allows us to learn more about the data before running any model and presenting the final visualization. There are many strengths to this form of exploratory visualization. These include identifying outliers, spotting any missing data, identifying significant variables and determining the size of the dataset.

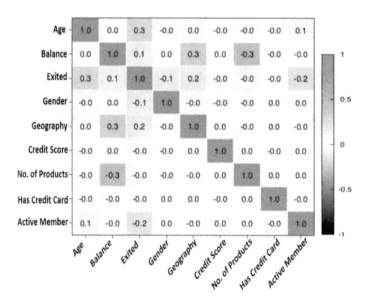

Figure 4.13: A correlation matrix table showing variation across a number of variables.

The first part of the analysis we carried out in this example explored some common types of data visualization techniques such as the count plot for categorical variable representation and the joint plot for representing bivariate variables. The distribution plot and the boxplot helps to explore the data further. Such techniques contain descriptive statistical information such as the mean median and interquartile range.

Figure 4.13 shows a correlation matrix showing the

coefficients between the variables, the number in each cell refers to the correlation between two variables, i.e. the one that is at the top of the column and the ones at the top of the row. A correlation value can be between -1 and 1, and it is the parameter that tells us about how connected these variables. Therefore, we can observe how a change in one variable related to the resulting change the other. Moreover, the more correlated the two variables are, the higher the correlation number (closer to 1) will be.

A correlation of 1 is ideal, which means the two variables considered are perfectly correlated with each other. Looking at Figure 4.13, one can observe the correlations of 1 along the diagonal. Similarly, a correlation value of 0 means the two variables are not correlated, and a negative correlation shows the two variables are related in an opposing manner. From the correlation matrix shown in Figure 4.13, it can be observed that the customer credit score and number of other products have no correlation while age, bank balance, gender and branch location have low correlations.

Clearly, further forms of analysis, such as logistic regression for binary classification, can well be performed on this sort of problems. Such analysis combined with visualization can prove to be very efficient, easy to interpret, and output well-calibrated predicted probabilities. However, its drawback is that this method does not work well in case of the non-linear problems – where the relationships between variables are often complex.

The main point of this example is to visually analyze a dataset and produce insight and to understand the data in question. It introduced a banking problem, utilized a dataset to run practical analysis to obtain insight into the problem of the churn rate.

Discussions

In data visualization, we are always looking to enhance the presentation of large quantities of data through the channels of visual communication. To do this, we usually start with a question. We then look for the appropriate dataset, to select a proportion of the data often from a large dataset, to help us answer that question. The choice of visualization technique or method must also be considered with great care. We are also looking for gaining insight or knowledge as we answer the crucial question. Hence, crafting a cohesive narrative around the key question and selecting the right data points to deliver the visual message is essential.

If we are to take two examples, one a drawing on a cave wall dating back millennia and the other a line graph projecting quarterly sales of a modern business, what could these two possibly have in common? Initially, it may appear somewhat absurd to compare these two examples. However, they are both telling a story. The cave drawings may have shown religious rituals, hunting techniques and social structures while the line graphs may illustrate a company thriving at one point and in financial stress the next.

Common examples of visualization are charts, graphs and maps but good visualizations are by far not restricted to them. The method of data visualization predominantly depends on what message one wants to convey. For example, to illustrate a comparison, one may utilize a line graph or a pie chart which will demonstrate several entities against one another in an attempt to find a pattern or a trend. Alternatively, to demonstrate a process, a flow chart would be better suited, which will demonstrate a task with the possibility of it being broken down further into sub-tasks. Another method which is increasingly utilized is geographical visualization such as bubble plots - which shows a scalable bubble over a location with a variable size depending on its value.

It would be inaccurate to state that one particular form of visualization is better than another as it is very much a case of comparing apples with oranges. However, there are more appropriate methods for the task at hand. For example, using a line graph to demonstrate the average population age for each country would suffice. However, there are currently more than 196 countries in the world. A solution to this would be a geographical chart which could use a colored scale to illustrate the very same point in a much cleaner illustration.

Additionally, to use a bar chart to demonstrate the market share price of energy companies would not paint a very understandable picture when one is concerned with comparing their share performances. A better a solution to this particular problem would be providing a percentage based pie chart which would clearly demonstrate which company holds the bigger share.

References

T. Edward, "Visual Explanations: Images and Quantities,

Evidence and Narrative", Graphics Press, Cheshire, CT, (1997).

D. W. Scott, "On Optimal and Data-based Histograms", Biometrika, 66(3), 605–610, (1979).

N. Kong, J. Heer, M. Agrawala, "Perceptual Guidelines for Creating Rectangular Treemaps", IEEE Transactions on Visualization and Computer Graphics, 16 (6), 990–8, (2010).

5

MULTIDISCIPLINARY EXAMPLES

Data visualization is a human-centric approach to examining data with the goal of gaining useful insight to support decision-making. In the present day, people rely heavily on visualization to gain insights into data and present results in an understandable form. Data visualization enables us to make it easier and faster to identify hidden relationships that exist in data.

Numbers do not lie, and graphs are the best representation of numbers to communicate the hidden story behind a set of numbers. Data visualization empowers reporters and researchers to communicate their findings to the stakeholders. Many visualization techniques and tools are used to perform comparative, relational, compositional or distribution analysis of data and to select the right visualization technique is vital or else the message may be left buried underneath the beautiful displays.

Understanding data is the first milestone that needs to be done before carrying out any form of analysis. However, to gain insight into what the numbers are trying to communicate is not possible without the help of descriptive statistics of the variables. Exploratory data analysis instigates the urge to learn about data and find the hidden patterns and information by using various data analysis approaches.

The discussion in this chapter aims to showcase some of the

methods, techniques and tools we discussed in the previous chapter. In this sense, we aim to show how data visualization can be utilized in real life. With the aid of a wide array of examples, in this chapter, we discuss data visualization in a multidisciplinary setting.

Visualizing World Happiness

The World Happiness Report is a key survey conducted by Helliwell et al., (Helliwell et al. 2019) looking at the global happiness level as perceived by citizens from 156 countries. The report was first published in 2015 and is continually updated every year. Attributes which are reported in the report include entities like GDP per capita, family, health (Life Expectancy), level of freedom, generosity, and the level of corruption (trust in the government). The report highlights the quantitative numbers for each of the chosen attributes of each country. As a result, it may become difficult to compare and contrast the happiness attributes globally in a visually appealing way.

To help visualize the global picture of the world happiness data, we utilize Chernoff faces. The main attributes chosen to visualize are,

- GDP per capita,
- family,
- health (Life Expectancy),
- generosity,
- level of corruption (trust in the government),
- and the overall happiness level.

In order to do this, using Chernoff's facial glyph model, data from the above attributes are normalized and are scaled to the range between 0 and 1. The following model attributes are then considered, as shown in Table 5.1.

Convexity of smile	Happiness level
Width of the Face	GDP per capita
Slant of eyebrows	Trust in the government
Length of the nose	Generosity
Size of the eyes	Health
Height of the face	Family

Table 5.1: Variables used in Chernoff's facial model for visualizing the world happiness.

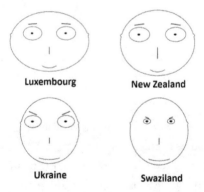

Figure 5.1: Chernoff's facial happiness visualization of the chosen attributes for some selected countries.

Figure 5.1. shows the Chernoff's facial happiness visualization of the chosen attributes for some selected countries of the world.

In this example, we are interested in comparing the happiness level, based on some chosen attributes. We are particularly interested in making a direct comparison between countries. In that sense, Chernoff's faces are a neat way to show the picture from the dataset.

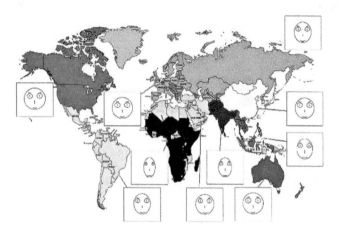

Figure 5.2: Chernoff's faces based on the average values for the chosen attribute for the continents of the world.

As one knows very well, countries around the world differ in the attributes representing the happiness level. As one can observe from the visualization shown in Figure 5.2, countries in the regions around North America, Australia, New Zealand and Western Europe appear to top the happiness score list and the countries from Sub-Sahara Africa, and Southern Asia are low on the happiness score.

Depression in California

This example is concerned with the understanding of the state of mental health among Californians. For this, we have utilized a dataset by Let's get Healthy California (LGHC) initiative. LGHC is an initiative which started in 2012 with the prime aim of making Californians mentally healthy through key health initiatives.

The dataset utilized here comes from HealthData.gov (HealthData.gov, 2019). It is a relatively concise dataset and comprises of records between 2012 and 2017 and has been published on the healthdata.gov website. This dataset reports figures among adults from ages 18 to 65 and over who are clinically diagnosed with depression. Key parameters available for comparison are gender, race, education, and income per annum of the participants.

The dataset was initially published as a means of creating awareness amongst the masses on the significant increase in mental illnesses in the state of California. This data can be used to draw several important conclusions with regard to clinical depression and possible implications as well as the shifting trends in the diagnosis. It can be utilized to show a visual representation of the state of mental health among Californians and the various trends of the illness.

In order to get an idea of the general trend in the data, standard visualization techniques can be utilized. In addition to this, data enrichment techniques such as a polynomial interpolation on the data can be carried out.

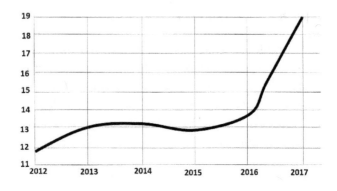

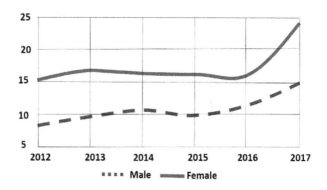

Figure 5.3: Percentage of Californians clinically diagnosed with depression between 2012 and 2017. This figure also shows the gender variation in terms of the percentage of Californians clinically diagnosed with depression between 2012 and 2017 — visualization of the general trend in the data using polynomial interpolation.

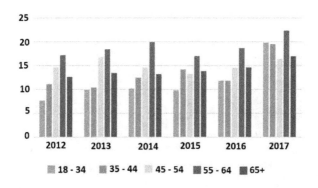

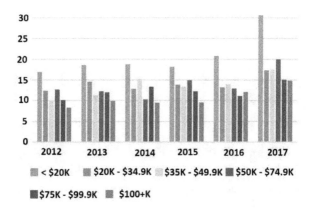

Figure 5.4: Bar graphs showing the variation of depression against age and income.

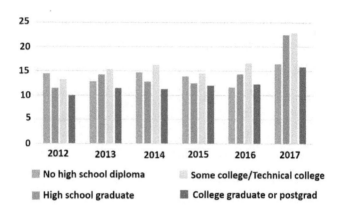

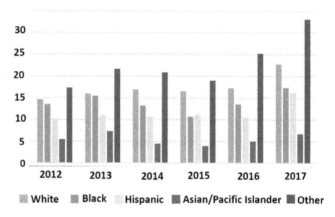

Figure 5.5: Bar graphs showing the variation of depression against education and ethnicity.

Figure 5.3 shows the percentage of Californians clinically diagnosed with depression. It also shows the gender variation of the percentage of Californians clinically diagnosed with depression between 2012 and 2017. This visualization shows how depression has consistently affected females than males in California during the period 2012 to 2017. Figures 5.4 and 5.5 provide further variations in visualization to show the status of depression cases in California for a chosen period of time.

The use of a polynomial based line graph clearly indicates increasing trends. The use of column bar graphs clearly shows other variations.

Rough Sleepers in England

Homelessness in the UK is defined as when someone has no home in the UK or anywhere else in the world available for them to live. It falls into many categories ranging from having no shelter to occupy to living in insecure dwellings. Rough sleeping is considered to be the most visible form of homelessness. People sleeping rough are at increased risk of being victims of violence.

Furthermore, rough sleepers are more likely to injure themselves deliberately. Therefore, it is important to know where resources should be deployed to alleviate rough sleeping. The Ministry of Housing, Communities and Local Government (MHCLG) publishes official statistics on the number of rough sleepers annually. (Gov.uk, 2019).

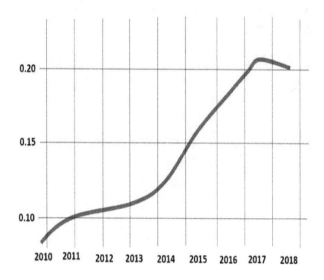

Figure 5.7: Number of rough sleepers per 1,000 households in England from 2010 to 2018.

In order to assess rough sleeping rates by the local authority, a combination of polynomial interpolation and choropleth maps can be used, as shown in Figures 5.7 and 5.8.

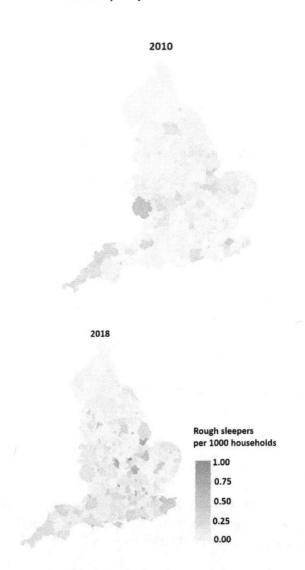

Figure 5.8: Choropleth map showing the number of rough sleepers in 2010 and 2018.

The visualizations show that the number of rough sleepers in England has increased between 2010 and 2018. It also shows that rough sleepers are not evenly distributed throughout England.

GDP Per Capita and National IQ

Intelligent Quotient (IQ) is widely regarded as one of the best predictors of success in today's society. This measure, therefore, can be an important indicator for a thriving society. In this sense, IQ can be integral to some government programs and academic research. For example, it is currently used in the United States as a predictor to determine if someone is fit for military services. This raises the question of whether IQ simply allows for a better socio-economic status or if it can be improved by supplementing the socio-economic status.

In an attempt to understand the relationship between IQ and the socioeconomic status, one could source appropriate data and attempt an analysis aided by visualizations. The data source for this example comes from the National IQ (Becker, 2019) along with the GDP per capita obtained from the World Bank (GDP Data, 2019). The national IQ dataset contains the IQ data from 203 countries, and the GDP per capita dataset contains the historical data of the GDP per capita of 264 countries from 1960 to 2018.

In order to analyze and visualize the data, a scatter plot approach is adopted. Thus, a scatter plot of GDP per capita is the independent variable and IQ being the dependent variable is plotted for the data. Here, one can use linear, exponential and logarithmic interpolations, as shown in Figures 5.9, 5.10 and 5.11, to draw conclusions.

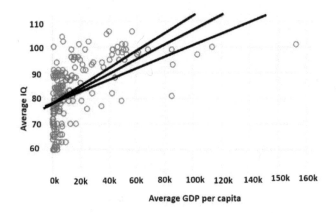

Figure 5.9: Linear interpolation on a scatter plot showing the relationship between GDP per capita and national IQ.

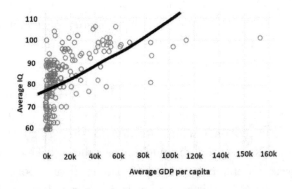

Figure 5.10: Exponential interpolation on a scatter plot showing the relationship between GDP per capita and national IQ.

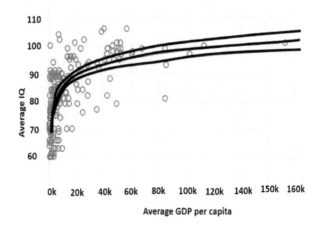

Figure 5.11: Logarithmic interpolations on a scatter plot showing the relationship between GDP per capita and national IQ.

Scatter plots are typically used in scientific visualization to see the relationship between two variables that may potentially be related. The main advantage of using scatter plots is the fact that a relationship can often be interpreted – through not proven - straight away as a result of the pattern of the plots.

As we can observe from Figure 5.9 and Figure 5.10, there appears to be a continuous relationship between the IQ and the socio-economic status. However, looking at Figure 5.11, one can suspect that this might not be the case. Hence the logarithmic interpolation rather than linear or exponential interpolation, in this case, provides a better understanding.

Fighting Styles of Michael Bisping

Michael Bisping is one of the renowned fighters in the Ultimate Fighting Championships (UFCs). He is the first British man to fight in a UFC main event and the sole British man who has won a UFC title. In sports analytics, the tactics and performances of players are analyzed often. This not only may help to improve the performance of the players but also helps to train other potential champions. In this instance, it may be interesting to look at some of the Bisping's attributes which he adopts in his fights.

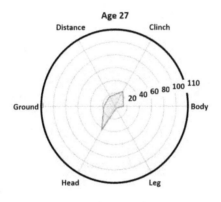

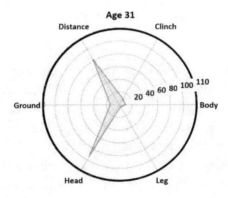

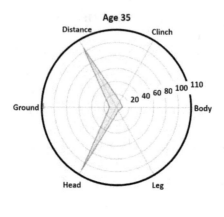

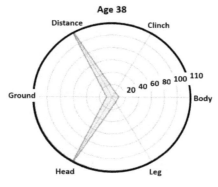

Figure 5.12: Michael Bisping's punch pattern variation across his age during the UFC fights.

UFC is a historical dataset between 1993 – 2019 of fight matches that have occurred in this tournament with the winner and loser (UFC Data, 2019). The dataset contains the player attributes of age, weight, height and reaches with fighting stance style and damage suffered and given. It has 5,144 rows and 145 columns of data representing the fighting match of two opponents with relevant features to the outcome of the competition. In this particular case, the interest is in Michael Bisping and therefore data relating to attributes which include his average attack scores towards, Body, Clinch, Distance, Ground, Head, and Leg were analyzed.

In order to visualize the results, Radar charts can be utilized. Radar charts are a type of glyph useful in comparing multiple physical attributes, as it allows readers to quickly visualize the general patterns in the data.

As can be seen from Figure 5.12, when Michael Bisping established his career in the UFC at the age of 27, his stats show he favored close clinch and head attacks. However, from age 28, he has shifted from the clinch to distance-based attacks. At age 29, he appeared to have started to strongly rely on distance and head attacks and rapidly improved these attributes all the way to the age of 38.

Rates of Cancer Incidents by Age and Gender

Cancer is considered to be the second leading cause of death in many parts of the world, including the United States. Roughly 14 million new cases of cancer were reported globally in 2012, with 8 million cancer-related deaths. By looking at past data, trends can be detected for certain groups of people, some more obvious than others, such as breast cancer in females.

In order to study the rates of cancer by age, we have chosen a suitable dataset from Cancer Registration: Cancer Incidence in England (1971-2016) (Cancer Dataset, 2019). This data is separated by year, age, gender, and the location of the tumor. Age is grouped into 5 year bands starting with 0-4 and 5-9 and ending with 90+ years. The tumor sites are coded. For example, code is ICD8 for years 1971 to 1978, ICD9 for years 1979 to 1994, and ICD10 for 1995 onwards.

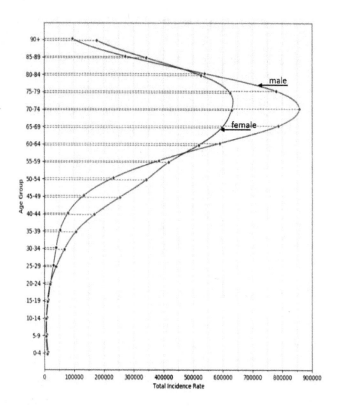

Figure 5.13: Total cancer incidences per age group between 1971 to 2016.

To visualize the data, here we have chosen the lollipop graphs. Lollipop graphs are chosen as it displays the positions of each point of data without adding too much unnecessary clutter to the visualization, whilst also allowing for easy comparison between bars. The lack of clutter, therefore, allows a smooth polynomial curve to be fitted for interpolation and to effectively visualize the variation.

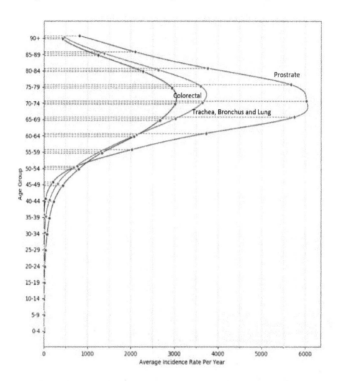

Figure 5.14: Average cancer incidence rates for males per year from 1995 to 2016.

The graph in Figure 5.13 shows how cancer becomes more likely as a person grows older, peaking at the age cluster 65 to 79, before dropping again. It is likely that it drops off here due to a drop in the living population at around this mark, as the typical lifespan is around 80, and therefore it can be argued that typically cancer incidences would otherwise continue rising through the age groups.

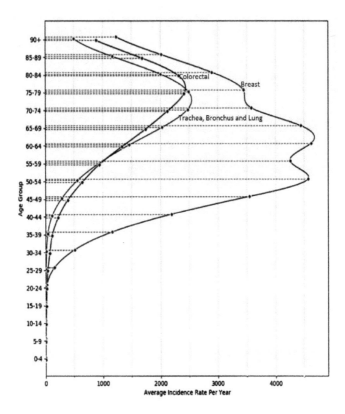

Figure 5.15: Average cancer incidence rates for females per year from 1995 to 2016.

In Figures 5.14 to 5.15, we use the average incidence rate per year for each age group rather than the total incidence. This is to make it more relevant for the reader to be able to easily see the likelihood of developing each type of cancer, based on their age and gender.

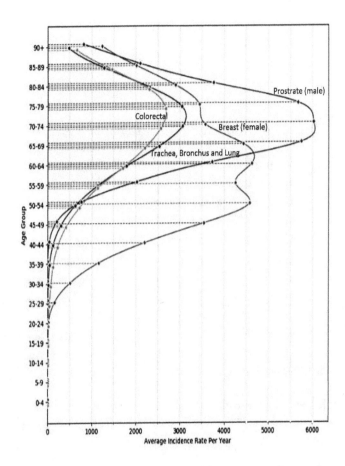

Figure 5.16: Average cancer incidence rates for males and females per year from 1995 to 2016.

The graphs above clearly demonstrate how cancer incidence has risen and changed across the years, with the primary cancer types staying on top with minor fluctuations. The age comparison lollipop plots make it clear to see how age affects the likelihood of each cancer, clearly displaying the age cluster 65 to 79 the most likely time to develop a common type of cancer, with the exception of breast cancer in females, which appears to be most common between the ages of 50 and 69.

Driver Age and Traffic Accidents

In this example, we visualize how road traffic accidents may be related to the age of the drivers. For this particular case of visualization, we have sourced a dataset comprising of road traffic accidents information occurred in Leeds UK in 2015 (Road Traffic Accidents, 2019). The dataset, having a total of fifteen attributes, consist of the location, number of people and vehicles involved, road surface, weather conditions, casualty class, age of casualty and gender of casualty. In order to do the analysis and visualization, we considered the casualty class (driver/rider, passenger or pedestrian), age of casualty and gender of the casualty within the dataset.

To visualize the data, we have utilized both the boxplot and density plot approach. The visualizations in graph form are shown in Figures 5.17 and 5.18.

A boxplot is an efficient graphical way of representing groups of numerical data using their quartiles. A boxplot graph can be used to visualize the five most significant values of a dataset such as the minimum value, the first quartile, the median, the third quartile, and the maximum value. In addition, boxplots can be utilized to point out the outliers in the data, i.e. the results of data outside the minimum and maximum values are considered outliers that can easily be determined from the box plot.

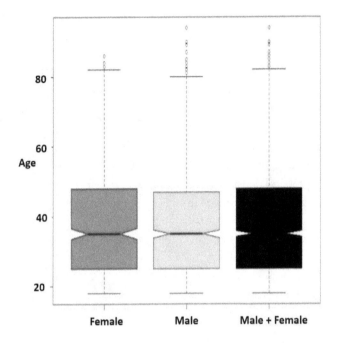

Figure 5.17: Boxplot visualization between traffic accidents and age.

On the other hand, a density plot is generally an effective way of looking at the distribution of a given set of variables. Visualization using density plots show the distribution of data over successive intervals or time intervals. It is also an effective alternative to a histogram that plots to allow a degree of data smoothing.

Looking at the visualization, the boxplot in Figure 5.17, we see no huge difference between female and male drivers. In the boxplot graph, the part corresponding to female and male, the median age of the driver is 35 years.

We also note that almost 50% of traffic accidents were by drivers in the age range between 34 and 48 years. By analyzing this area in more detail, in comparison with others, for the age range between 25 and 35 years, the distribution appears to be more compact and intense, and the density plot confirms this. Thus, though the great majority of the traffic accidents are caused by drivers aged between 35 and 48 years, the peak of this distribution is for the ages between 25 and 35 years. Thus, a combination of boxplot and density plot, in this case, has helped to visualize the data and draw more meaningful conclusions.

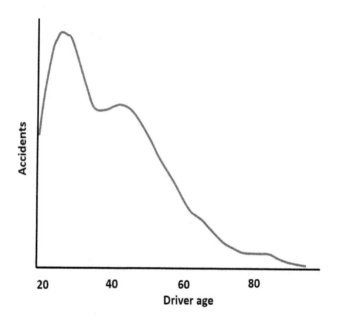

Figure 5.18: Density plot visualization between traffic accidents and age.

Seeing the UK Gender Pay Gap

In the UK, employers with 250 or more employees are required to reveal the employment figures which can show the gender pay gap. The issue of gender pay inequality is a much-debated matter. The issue appears to be as lively as today since it started over 100 years back with the first wave of feminism in the world.

To understand the full extent of the pay gap, and if this claim is true, it is important to visualize and analyze the data, comparing female and male pay in the same jobs so comparison and conclusion can be drawn. The data we have used in these examples are drawn from the Government Equalities Office (Gender Pay Gap, 2019). The attributes of this data include male/female bonuses, lower quartile, middle quartile and upper quartile.

The points of interest here are,

- do women get paid less than men,
- do men and women receive equal bonuses,
- and does the skill level of the job affect the pay gap?

We use the data to do boxplot visualizations in order to analyse and draw conclusions. A boxplot is a five number summary visualization with the maximum, third quartile, median, first quartile and the minimum. This can be used to calculate the interquartile range, which is the third quartile minus the first quartile.

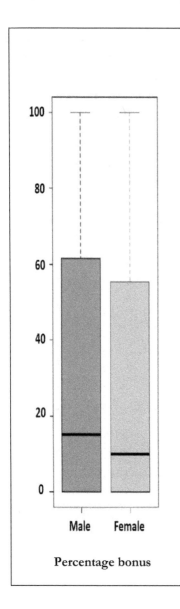

This plot shows the bonus percentage for male and female employees for 150 companies that were used in the analysis. The upper whisker on both male and female boxplots is equal, suggesting that the top bonus is paid equally to both male and female employees.

However, the median and the upper quartile are noticeably lower for female employees. This could be due to a number of reasons, i.e. the data does not tell us how the bonuses are awarded or the male/female ratio within the companies. All aspects need to be studied to draw a meaningful conclusion.

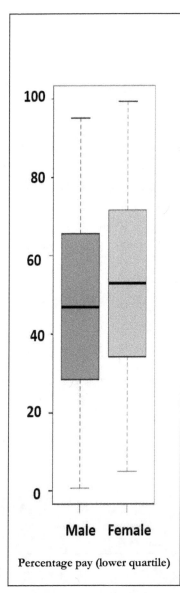

Percentage pay (lower quartile)

This plot shows the distribution of pay for lower skilled workers. It can be clearly seen that females are getting paid more on average compared to males of the same skillset.

This could again be due to many factors such as more women being in lower skilled jobs or due to women less likely to receive promotions due to the style of work. This would require a more detailed dataset, for example, information on the ratio at distinct skill levels.

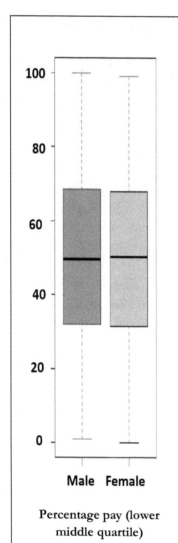

Male   Female

Percentage pay (lower middle quartile)

The plot from the lower middle quartile suggests that the male and female employees have equal pay or are closer to each other.

However, again, in order to draw meaningful conclusions, this cannot be looked at in isolation. It is crucial to look at other aspects of the data.

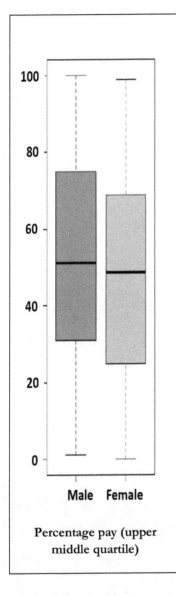

Percentage pay (upper middle quartile)

The upper middle quartile shows men being paid slightly more, and this is the first skill of workers we see whereby men are paid slightly more.

Depending on what is classed as an 'Upper Middle' skill job, the pay gap could be due to many factors, promotions, societal encouragement to study towards a top degree, maternity leave (falling behind on the career ladder) etc.

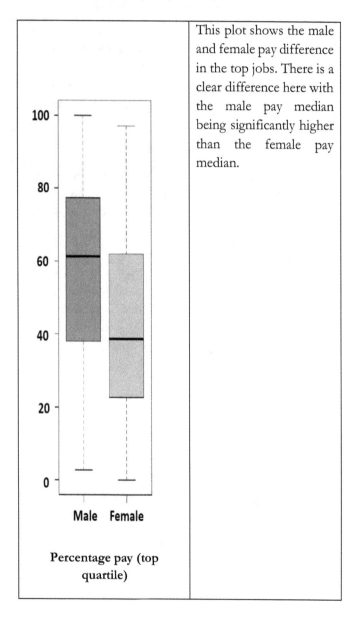

This plot shows the male and female pay difference in the top jobs. There is a clear difference here with the male pay median being significantly higher than the female pay median.

Percentage pay (top quartile)

As for the example discussed here, from the data that is analyzed and visualized, it is apparent that there is a gender pay gap particularly in the higher paid jobs and it is also noticeable that male employees get paid higher bonuses than their female colleagues.

However, data analysis and visualization must be used with caution when drawing important conclusions. For a complete picture, data size and other crucial attributes may well be required to see the full and complete picture.

Visualizing Crime Hotspots using Point Mapping

Criminal activities are usually randomly distributed over space. Criminal activities tend to concentrate in certain places because of the relative interaction between victims and offenders and the strength of policing. Areas of concentrated crime are often referred to as hotspots. Researchers and police use the term "hotspots" in many different ways to often refer to areas of concentrated crime.

Hotspot mapping is a popular spatial analytical technique used by law enforcement, police and crime reduction agencies to visually identify where crime tends to be highest, helping decision-makers to determine where to target and deploy their resources. Though no common definition of the term hotspot of crime exists, the common understanding is that a hotspot is an area that has a greater than the average number of criminal or disorderly events. It can also be identified as areas where people have a higher than average risk of being victimized. A clearly identified and accurately visualized crime hotspot map will significantly help in the prediction and prevention of crimes.

In this example, we represent the locations of the crimes that happened in Bradford UK in 2016. This would give us an idea of the distribution of the crimes in the area, and it can lead to a possible hypothesis about the spatial distribution of them. The chosen dataset used in this study comes from UK police website data.police.uk. The dataset contains information about every single crime that UK police encountered. The data comes in easy to use CSV file format, and it has criminal records across Bradford for the period 1 January 2016 to 31 December 2016. The dataset gives the crime type, the month of occurrence of the crime along with the exact geographic location. In total, it is composed of 12 attributes with 73,598 instances.

The analysis of point patterns is the study of the spatial distribution of points in 2 or 3-dimensional space. The area to be considered may be referred to as a point pattern. The point pattern is a stochastic process in which we observe the locations of some events of interest within a bounded region.

Point mapping can be used for identifying hotspots of crime. This is because of the ease of its use to spatially understand the size and location of the crimes. It also helps to map the orientation of clusters of crime incidents. In particular, there are two main issues of interest, the distribution of events in space and the existence of possible interactions between them. Crimes as points on a map can be aggregated to the geographic unit areas. These areas can then be shaded in accordance with the number of crimes that fall within them. Furthermore, this method enables the user to determine which areas have a high incidence of crime in a short period of time. In addition, census areas can easily be linked with other data sources, such as population, to calculate a crime rate, increasing their versatility for analysis.

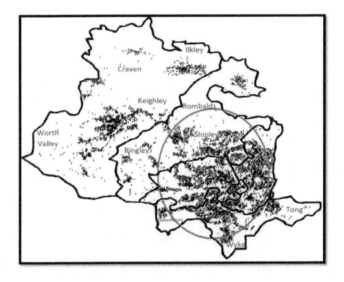

Figure 5.19: Point data map for the distribution of crimes in Bradford UK in 2016.

Figure 5.19 shows the distribution of crimes on the Bradford map using the point-mapping method. The region marked with a circular boundary is the mean center. It is identified to be the mean value of longitude and the mean value of latitude, and the region marked by the circle is the standard distance which provides us with the visual view on the spread of our data around the mean center.

The biggest crime hotspots in Bradford are generally located around the city center. It is normal for many city centers to have high incidents of crime. Another crime hotspot which can be identified here is Keighley in the west of Bradford.

Point mapping is an efficient method to visualize data, and it is helpful for those who patrol and investigate crimes by simply indicating where incidents have occurred. It is a suitable approach for displaying geographic patterns of crimes, especially for mapping individual crimes and small volumes of crimes. It can also be used to report repeat locations through the use of graduating symbol sizes. Using this method makes it easier to identify and analyze the hotspots (clusters) that we obtain from our point map. By using data from the past, point mapping identifies where crimes will most densely concentrate in the future, which will help in crime prevention and reduction.

24 Years of Wildfires in the United States

This example concerns the study of wildfires in the US over the period 24 years, i.e. between 1992 and 2015. Wildfires - also called wildland fires - burn a million miles of land every year in the US at speeds up to 14 miles per hour that spread the flames quickly over land. They are classified into three main types depending on the form of vegetation in which the fire occurs. They are forest fires, brush and peat fires. They are most common in the US when compared to other areas because of the combination of heat, drought and strong winds. In this example, the aim is to discover the possible patterns of wildfires for each US state by analyzing and visualizing the wildfire records.

The dataset used for this visualization is available on Kaggle

(US Wildfires, 2019). The dataset contains the third update of publication for 1.88 million records of US wildfires over the period of 24 years, from 1992 to 2015. The wildfire records were acquired from federal or other local fire organizations. The dataset includes 39 attributes that discriminate each wildfire in terms of date, size, cause, state, coordinates and other fire specific codes such as fire size class and date of the fire control.

The dataset has more than 1.8 million records that can be combined to extract useful knowledge such as the dates, the cause or the size of the wildfires. However, similar research has been conducted on individual features, and it would be trivial to examine the same ones or to draw similar, or the same conclusions, such as that wildfires are more frequent in the summer months when the temperatures are higher with more sunlight hours per day.

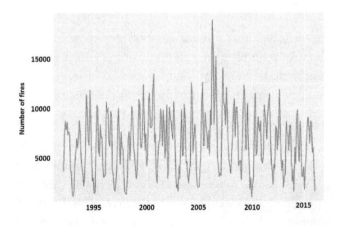

Figure 5.20: Linear interpolation showing the monthly variation on fire incidences over the 24-year period.

Although the dataset is time-dependent for millions of records, simple linear interpolation and bar graphs may help to visualize and analyze the data.

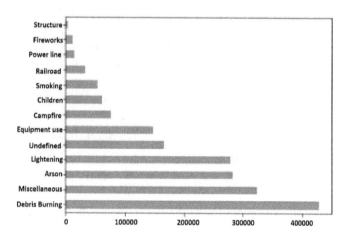

Figure 5.21: Bar graph visualization of causes of wildfires.

Figure 5.20 shows a linear interpolation of the dataset to show the monthly variations on fire incidences over the 24-year period. From the plot, it is clear that there were particularly high incidents of fire across the country over the period between 2005 and 2010.

From Figure 5.21, it is clear that that Debris Burning is the most common origin of wildfires, followed by Miscellaneous, Arson and Lightning, while Structure, Fireworks and Power line are the least common. Figure 5.22 shows the top 20 states in which wildfires happened whereby, California (CA), Georgia (GA) and Texas (TX) are in the first three positions while Wisconsin and Arizona (AR) are in 19th and 20th positions.

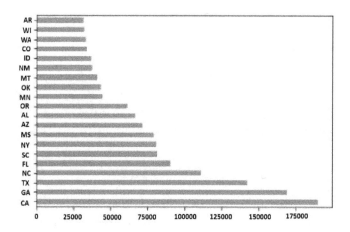

Figure 5.22: Bar graph visualizing the 20 most prominent states with wildfires.

Wildfires and natural disasters, in general, can destroy natural resources crucial for human existence and survival of the humankind. In this example, we have explored a dataset with records of 24 years of wildfires in the US, in order to find patterns successfully for wildfire origins for each state and consequently try to reduce and eliminate the disastrous effects of them for the future.

The visualization technique used is horizontal bar graphs selected for their effectiveness and to draw attention to the importance of the situation. For the analysis part, linear interpolation is used after the transformation of the dataset in monthly intervals for better evaluation of the representation. Further analysis of the dataset would be beneficial for predicting the causes of wildfires in the future, using machine learning algorithms and with the appropriately matched visualizations.

Bike Renting in Washington, DC

With the increase in the number of motor vehicles on our roads today, air pollution has been increasing steadily and significantly. Creating innovative models to facilitate the usage of bikes would motivate people to use alternative and environmentally friendly forms of transportation instead of cars whenever it is possible.

In this example, we analyse and discuss bike renting in Washington, DC, using a dataset on Kaggle (Bike Sharing Demand, 2019). The data represents records of rented bikes for different days and weather conditions in Washington, DC. This dataset contains 10,887 records of bike rental information for a two-year period between 2011 and 2012. Moreover, it includes 12 attributes: date, time, season, holiday, working day, temp, atemp (average temperature), humidity, wind speed, casual registered, and count.

Based on the dataset and given its attributes, the targeted question to be discussed and analyzed is, what is the correlation between the number of rented bikes and attributes such as temperature, weather, season, day time, holiday and working day? To answer this question and do some analysis upon this question, one can adopt the method of correlation.

Correlation represents a method for extracting common characteristics from data pairs which then can be used to learn and see more information about the dataset. This technique is essentially a linear approach to data analysis and visualization, and since the dataset is not very complex, in this case, the correlation may be an appropriate method to adopt to obtain some insights on the relationship between the variables considered. If two variables are correlated, it can be said that there is a regular change in one variable and in the other one as well.

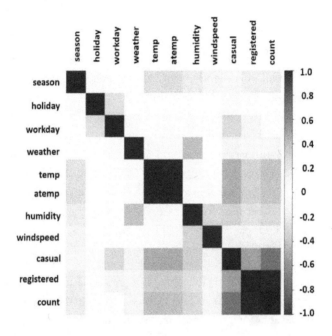

Figure 5.23: Corrplot showing the correlation between the data attributes for bike rental.

In this case, we want to see how the number of rented bikes will change based on temperature, or weather conditions, season, working days and holidays. Correlation between variables can be negative if one variable increases, and the other decreases, and positive when both variables increase at the same time. Therefore, 1 represents the strongest positive correlation, while -1 represents the strongest negative correlation, and 0 represents no correlation between the data.

In Figure 5.23, the scale of correlation represented is from -1 to -1. From these values, we are interested in monitoring the correlation of count, the number of rented bikes, with other attributes such as temp, season, working day and holiday.

By looking at Figure 5.23, we can see that the number of rented bikes is slightly positively correlated with the season attribute. Since the season attribute falls in categorical data type, the correlation between count and season is quite vague and difficult to quantify. Furthermore, we can see that there is almost no correlation between count versus holiday, and count versus working days. Therefore, the correlation method is not suitable to find the connection between these variables because, in this case, the working days and holidays are categorical data denoted by 0 and 1.

However, if we look at the temp versus count, we can observe some valuable information about the correlation between these variables since both have numerical representation and mathematical meaning behind. From the figure, we can see that count and temp are positively correlated. Therefore, we can infer that higher temperatures indicate the increasing number of rented bikes.

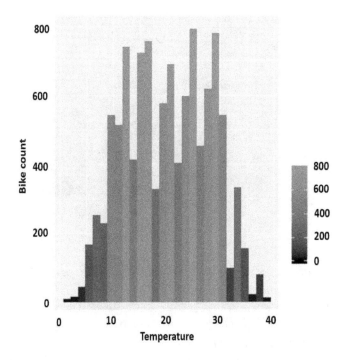

Figure 5.24: Histogram plot showing the correlation between bike count and the temperature attribute.

Other variables, such as casual and registered, which are highly correlated with count attribute, represent the number of non-registered and registered users of bikes. Therefore, obviously, the correlation between these variables and the count variable is high. From the chosen dataset, the best understanding comes from the connection and correlation between the number of bikes and temperature.

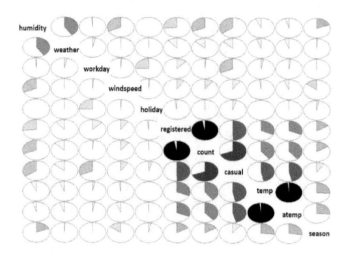

Figure 5.25: Corgram plot showing the correlation between the data attributes for bike rental.

Figure 5.24 depicts the relationship between temperature and rented bikes. It can easily be seen that in very low temperatures and very high temperatures the number of rented bikes decreases significantly, whereas, in the temperatures between 10 and 30 degrees of Celsius, the number of rented bikes is significantly higher.

Thus, the correlation method gives us good information about the relation between temperature and the number of rented bikes. These two variables are positively correlated with the value equal to 0.394453645. However, the correlation between bike count and other attributes such as working days, holidays and seasonal attributes is quite vague because these attributes fall into a categorical data type. Even though these attributes are denoted with a range of numbers, 0 to 1 and 1 to 4, there is no mathematical meaning of these values. Therefore, when working with categorical data, the classification technique is more appropriate for data analysis.

Figure 5.25 depicts another visualization technique using the 'corgram' plot for representing the correlation between bike count and the rest of the attributes. As can be seen from Figure 5.25, the correlation between variables of our dataset is represented by multiple pie charts. In comparison with the first method of visualization represented in Figure 5.23, from this technique, even though equally accurate, it can be harder to understand and interpret the results. Nonetheless, these techniques may also be useful at times for presenting the kind of data discussed in this example.

In this example, we have discussed the visualization of bike rental dataset, which represents the number of rented bikes within a two-year period in Washington, DC. The main goal of this example is to shed some light into the relationship between bike counts and other attributes recorded in the dataset such as temperature, season, working days and holidays. Furthermore, the visualization techniques used here describe the correlation between these variables.

From the results, it is inferred that there is a positive correlation between the number of rented bikes and temperature. Moreover, it is difficult to accurately describe the relationship between the number of rented bikes and the attributes such as holidays, working days and seasonal attributes because they were categorical data represented by a range of numbers with no mathematical meaning. However, it can be concluded that the correlation method and visualization techniques in the chosen dataset give us an important understanding of the dataset and the problem at hand. For better results (and perhaps for better visualizations) the dataset used in this example can be further analyzed by using regression and classification techniques.

Obesity Rates in England

In recent decades, with the development of food industrialization, obesity has become a major threat to human health. Obesity can lead to heart disease, diabetes, cancer and some mental illnesses such as depression. The UK is consistently in the top five of obesity rate in Europe. Britain spends £6 billion a year on treatment for obesity-related conditions. The British government published guidelines on healthy living and tackling obesity in 2011. Since then, a series of government policies aimed at reducing obesity have been launched, including putting calorie information on the menu and introducing a sugar tax.

This example looks at the number of primary or secondary diagnosis of obesity in people in England from 2006/07 to 2016/17, based on data from the NHS Digital (Data and Information, 2019). Different parameters such as gender and age were used to compare the growth rate of obesity in the population, to explore the effect of government policies on the increase of obesity rate in different periods. The data for this decade include two important points in time - the introduction of the calorie labelling policy in 2011 and the sugar tax in 2015. Although the sugar tax was only officially implemented in 2018, major beverage companies began to improve the product formula in 2015 to prepare for the introduction of sugar tax and do market research.

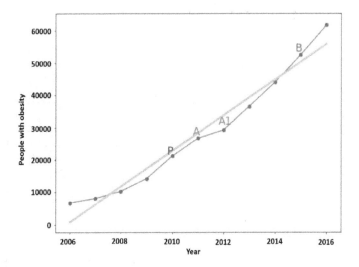

Figure 5.26: Line graph showing the rate of obesity growth - using data of people diagnosed with primary or secondary conditions of obesity.

In this example, for data visualization of the obesity dataset, we have utilized line graphs. Line graphs can obviously compare the growth rates using the slope of the selected line segment.

Figure 5.26 is a graph showing the trend in the total number of obese patients admitted to the hospital during the period of study. This graph clearly shows the change in the growth trend. One can clearly see that the gradient of the line segment AA1 is smaller than the line segment before the point A. Furthermore, the gradient of the line PA is also smaller than the line segment before the point P. The gradient of the line after the point B is almost the same as that of the line A1B. These results show a slight drop in obesity after 2010 and a further drop in 2011, but the growth has steadily started increasing after 2015.

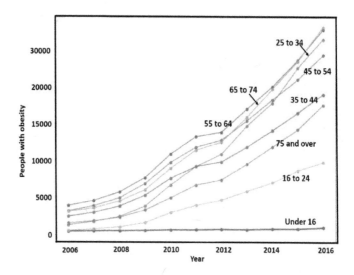

Figure 5.27: Line graphs showing the rate of obesity growth by age group - using data of people diagnosed with primary or secondary conditions of obesity.

Figure 5.27 shows a visual breakdown of obesity figures in terms of age groups. There were some interesting findings one can observe from this figure. The result for the under 16 age group is, for example, completely different from the rest of the age groups. Unlike the stability of obesity observed for children and teenagers, the number of obese people aged between 25 to 34 had a massive rise in the 10 years. This age group has some very distinctive characteristics, i.e., they just graduated from college, just started to work, began to gradually face a variety of life problems related to such things as finance and relationships.

Obesity is a global problem in the 21st century. Just like the environmental crisis, it is an acute problem that human societies are facing today. The calorie labelling policy was introduced in 2011 to successfully slow down the increase in obesity rates, but unfortunately, it did not last. The sugar tax has not had the desired effect at all. It shows that, in general, people are unlikely to stop eating unhealthy food simply because of the introduction of a government policy. Furthermore, in general, junk food is cheaper and therefore, it is affordable and convenient for people to consume.

We must also note that there are probably many reasons relating to people making the unwise decision to consume unhealthy food that gives rise to obesity. It is equally important to think about these related reasons that are causing the obesity crisis — for example, lifestyle, mental health and the level of earning probably play crucial roles too.

References

J. Helliwell, R. Layard, and J. Sachs, World Happiness Report, New York: Sustainable Development Solutions Network, https://worldhappiness.report, (2019).

HealthData.gov, https://healthdata.gov/ (2019).

Homelessness: Applying All Our Health. [Online] Available at:

https://www.gov.uk/government/publications/homeless
ness-applying-all-ourhealth/homelessness-applying-all-our-
health, [Accessed 2018].

D. Becker, The NIQ-Dataset (V1.3.3), Chemnitz, Germany,
(2019).

GDP Data, per capita (current US$), [Online] Available at:
https://data.worldbank.org/indicator/NY.GDP.PCAP.C
D?view=chart [Accessed 2019].

UFC Data, UFC-Fight historical data from 1993 to 2019.
[online] Available at:
https://www.kaggle.com/rajeevw/ufcdata [Accessed
2019].

Cancer Dataset, Cancer Registration: Cancer Incidence in
England (1971-2016), Public Health England, [Online]
https://data.gov.uk/dataset/3001390c-e3bb-460b-b5e5-
c726dd2fb3b8/cancer-registration-cancer-incidence-in-
england-1971-2016 [Accessed 2019].

Road Traffic Accidents, Leeds City Council, [Online]
https://data.gov.uk/dataset/6efe5505-941f-45bf-b576-
4c1e09b579a1/road-traffic-accidents [Accessed, 2019]

Gender Pay Gap, Government Equalities Office, [Online]
Government Equalities Office,
https://data.gov.uk/dataset/54219db1-dd98-49d9-a383-
a5978bb0aeb9/gender-pay-gap [Accessed, 2019].

US Wildfires, 1.88 Million US Wildfires, [Online] Kaggle,
https://www.kaggle.com/rtatman/188-million-us-
wildfires/kernels [Accessed, 2019].

Bike Sharing Demand, Kaggle, [Online],
https://www.kaggle.com/c/bike-sharingdemand/data
[Accessed, 2019].

Data and Information, NHS Digital, [Online]
https://digital.nhs.uk/ [Accessed, 2019].

6

CONCLUSIONS

Data visualization dates back to 2500 BC, where clay tablets were used to present information, generally of administrative or financial nature. In the 10th century, an original line graph was used to plot planetary movements where the x-axis represented days of the month, and the y-axis represented the position of the planets in the sky. In the 19th century, there was a visualization of the Paris to Lyon train timetable created where the x-axis represented hours of the day, and the y-axis showed the distance along the route.

Data visualization, thus, is not an entirely new topic. It has a long history. In this sense, it was widely used prior to the 17th century. People mainly recorded and utilized information on maps and resources by visualization. In the 18th century, more ways of data visualization came about. For example, William Playfair invented the most popular graphical visualizations that we use today. These include the line, bar, circle, and pie charts. Moreover, time series plots, contour plots, rose charts, and scatterplots also appeared in this period. By the 20th century, statistical visualization encountered a roadblock, because statisticians were concerned with images and were demanding accuracy, and they preferred to focus on exact numbers.

Afterwards, with the advent of computers, data visualization has become more accessible, to produce more accurate and plausible visualizations. However, as the technique of information visualization entered an era of big data, new challenges have emerged. It is not only that traditional statistical visualization is not sufficient for emerging technical requirements, but also the cultivation of talents and computing technology, such as cloud computing and quantum computing, need to improve.

Data visualization is the effective communication of complex ideas with precision, clarity and efficiency. A useful visualization allows one to see patterns, trends and insights which may otherwise go unnoticed. Any practical dataset contains a multitude of information. However, if the data is not often appropriately visualized, then, essential insights may go missing. Data visualization allows aspects of data to be highlighted, and in many ways, tells convincing stories backed with facts.

Today, data is being generated in high volumes. Exploring this data to find patterns and trends are becoming increasingly difficult due to the high volume. Data visualization helps with the management of this data, and upon successful completion, it answers questions. For the process of collecting and exploring data to be useful, one must take into account the visualization aspect – combining the creativity and general knowledge held by a human being with the computational storage capacity and power available today.

Over the years, data visualization has developed in such a way that it can be used to present and understand data in more accessible ways. This allows for faster data processing as well as assisting data scientists to see trends or anomalies in the data much faster than they would do if they were analyzing the data manually. The advancements in technology and the increased use of technological devices, have led to a surge in the production of data (big data). Consequently, companies and industries have come to realize that this data provides insightful knowledge that they can use. Big data is now a rapidly evolving industry which requires the use of data/information visualization. Here visualization is used to display facts in a way which is understandable and useful to a human working in any discipline.

The Question of Big Data

There is no definitive definition of big data, with each organization and body having their own twist to it. However, generally, it is a very large dataset, with the three Vs - volume, velocity and variety. Thus, devising visualization tools for data comes with many challenges and intricacies. Big data visualization is a field that is rapidly evolving due to its recent emergence and the continued exponential growth of complex multidimensional data. In order to handle the amount of data being generated, adequate visualization techniques are required for effective analysis of such datasets.

Big data originated as a way to describe sets of data that had become too large to be dealt with by traditional database systems. It has since become a term to encompass the data and the technologies used to deal with large collections of data for solving real-world problems.

Visualizing big data has only emerged at the turn of the 20th century as statistical computing slowly became a reality. Even so, for many individuals and organizations, the cost of visualizing and analyzing this data outweighed the benefit. As such, until this period, big data techniques were widely used just as a storage methodology. It was not until the 21st century that the processing power was cheap enough for it to be widely profitable.

In order to tackle the visualization challenges presented by big data, entirely new toolsets were required to be developed. Microsoft, Google and Amazon, for example, are all attempting to become major players in the space. The large amounts of data available results in the need for it to be processed beforehand. This involves tasks such as feature selection, wherein an "area" of the data is targeted to tackle a specific issue. This said, analyzing, for example, Twitter feeds without feature selection would provide nothing worthwhile. Real-time data sources, despite being a challenge, allow for the data to be visualized as it flows in. This is a more familiar reality, for example, with the emergence of the Internet of Things (IoT) devices.

When visualizing big data, there are various aims one must fulfil. They include identifying hidden patterns to allow for ease of searching for specific information, comparing the difference in quantities between data units and enabling user interaction. As big data can come in any form, it can be visualized in many ways. Standard methods such as bar charts, line graphs, histograms, and so on are still applicable. However, it may lose usefulness as the dataset grows. Therefore, a variety of image-based techniques are becoming popular, which involves techniques such as heat maps, word clouds and motion charts.

For example, the London bus system, in 2011, had in access of 2.3 billion passengers. Therefore, visualizations in the form of text feed for journeys as well as maps were carried out. It is possible to see the frequency and location of trips and infer patterns on passenger behavior and adjust bus routes. When used alongside the traffic maps, this data becomes even more powerful.

As highlighted, big data is useful when visualized as it can give a wide range of analysis in a variety of dimensions. This is becoming very valuable to big corporations who are increasingly trying to analyse user trends and predicting future behavior. Manual analysis to infer insights from these datasets may be too time-consuming.

Thus, the full adoption of big data has paved the way for visualizations as a primary analysis tool as it is the most effective way to gather useful insight. This results in the visualization frontier being moved forward at a more progressive rate and big investments being made in the field. This is supported by the fact that the big data industry is projected to be worth 123.2 billion USD by 2025.

Although big data visualization is powerful, it is still not widely available. Due to the significant costs involved with cloud storage and the processing power required in order to continually create visualizations of a dataset, visualizing big data is still an expensive task. As well as this, the variety of big data means that picking the perfect visualization method is not always straightforward.

Furthermore, due to the depth of information available

from a big data source, skewing this information becomes easy. This means that a malicious actor can manipulate big data to fit their own motives, creating misleading visualizations that can portray the data in a fashion that it otherwise is.

Visualizing big data is a difficult task that comes with many challenges. These challenges are continuing to grow year-on-year, meaning that constant evolution of the tools is required to keep up with the high demands. Volume, velocity and variety are continuing to prove to be big focuses, with velocity being the up comer as IoT devices become more common. Big data will be at the forefront of data science as all major corporations look to involve big data systems into their operations.

Big data visualizations hold major power within analytics, whilst benefitting the big players the most. This means that whilst the power is there when it is only in the hands of those who already possess it. These bodies may be the same ones who are more likely to abuse the easy manipulability of the data. However, as the field progresses, smaller players are becoming more involved at a smaller scale.

For further progress, it is essential that big data is continued to be posed as an analytical tool and not to push profit margins. Open-source foundations are the most definite way to ensure this, with plenty already existing within the big data analytics field. It is also essential that big data is pushed more within education as it is beginning to become a career of its own with distinct challenges compared to traditional data methods. Finally, the development of more thorough rules in terms of publishing data to reduce the occurrence of misleading statistics may prove helpful.

Challenges

The low latency data processing capacity is identified to be more crucial than before because big data are evolving rapidly. Traditional methods of data visualization have limitations when it comes to the analysis and visualization of big and complex data.

One of the challenges in data visualization is the ability to narrow the knowledge gap. With the abundance of data, this task has become challenging. Most data scientists are often not trained professionally for data visualization. They often rely on traditional visualization tools such as Microsoft Office tools or some graphical processing tools to generate simple tables and plot charts. These simple charts could not explain in detail the information about big data and affect people's understanding of such data. Thus, the lack of talent is one of the factors that restrict the development of data visualization as a field. Furthermore, the data analyst is a highly demanding profession. They need to have many years of related professional analysis experience and mathematical abilities. These abilities are difficult to develop in a short period of time. At the same time, the demands in this field are very high. In the USA, for example, there exist over 140,000 positions in big data analysis.

Poor functional performance and low expansibility are often inherent in many big data visualization tools. The reason is that big data is large in size and is large in dimension. The current data visualization tools are usually not efficient enough to handle such vast quantities of data. These uncertainties can affect the accuracy of results and the quality of viewing. In addition, another challenge is the format and type of data. Some data formats are not universal and can only be read or created using specific software. These formats could also cause data analysts to spend more time learning and fiddling with these visualization tools. Moreover, some types of data could be difficult to handle from a data visualization point of view. For example, the data with visual noise is complicated to separate or abstract due to the relativity of this data.

The lack of diversified visualization software also challenges the development of data visualization. At present many visualization tools are provided in the academic realm, but many academics are dependent on fewer forms of data analysis software that are not used by many organizations. It can cause hindrance in the communication of information. It is, therefore, considered to be a significant challenge.

Another challenge is on the accuracy and authenticity of the data sources themselves. Currently, many original sources of the datasets are heterogeneous. These data are often noisy and imperfect. For instance, some data can be integrated, transformed or reduced. It would change the result of the visualization.

Ethics Consideration

Many forms of data visualization are widely used to convey messages from a visual representation of information to an audience regardless of the background of the individuals. They are used in a wide variety of sectors and disciplines both in academia and industry, and their formation becomes more accessible and more comfortable with software replacing handwriting nowadays.

Therefore, ethics and data governance should always be considered in visualization, as different unintended conclusions, meanings and misconceptions might occur from the same data-graphic interpretations. In addition, ethical challenges deriving from societal differences, such as demographic and economic changes, might have significant consequences which must always be borne in mind. For example, unethical data visualizations have been abundant throughout the history of mankind - people have been misguided, purposefully or not, by false or fake graphs and plots, with vital information that is often missed out.

The first official regulation from EU regarding the processing of personal data and the movement of such data was in 1995, with the European Data Protection Directive (Directive 95/46/EC), even though Guidelines on the Protection of Privacy and Trans-Border Flows of Personal Data from the Organization for Economic Co-operation and Development (OECD) were adopted in 1980. From 25th of May in 2018, the General Data Protection Regulation (GDPR) is in force, which reinforces existing rights and establishes new forms for individuals such as the right to erasure from an organization if your personal data are no longer necessary for their original purpose.

Ethics in data visualization start long before the creation of the data representation. Initially, the chosen dataset should come from a reliable and trustworthy source, and decisions cannot be derived from biased data. Moreover, data analysis involves a lot of preprocessing, cleaning and outlier removal where data can be manipulated. Any assumptions taken during this process should be stated, and the procedure followed should be repeatable. Additionally, the design of the presentation should be driven by honesty, and accurate results rather than the effectiveness of the argument made.

Ethics and utility are vital factors for data visualization not only in data sciences but also in other sciences such as physics, and scientists often have to deal with such challenges especially when research has been conducted on a sensitive subject. Health data and more specifically, genetic data is one of the most discussed examples balancing risks and benefits of privacy and discrimination. The "right to science" is considered for data-intensive research both in biomedical and public health.

From the data governance perspective, data quality, security, sourcing and analytic definitions are only some of the tools and practices that should be followed for risk assessment minimization, efficient decision-making and long-term organizational success concerning data.

A data governance framework for managing information, data standardization and definitions of communication and authorization is critical for the success of an organization and especially when dealing with big data. For instance, the Recommendations on Health Data Governance from the

Organization for Economic Co-operation and Development (OECD) prioritizes health benefits over data sharing.

With the European Union's GDPR in force from 2018, a plethora of new suggestions have been derived regarding the advances in healthcare that can be made via data sharing. This often provides a probabilistic approach to a possible disease that needs further research. Under the regulations of security and privacy, similar health cases can be identified in different countries unanimously that previous legislation would not have allowed. Data visualizations can provide fast and secure solutions in this area and contribute to human knowledge and understanding.

At the other end of the spectrum, there is a wide variety of cases in which data sharing would not provide any additional benefit apart from data exploitation for commercial purposes and compromise ethics in the name of revenue - for example, insurance companies that are interested in customers' health data or even worse, genetic data could put revenue before ethics. Data governance in the organizations should include all these cases that contradict the regulations and should take action against them.

The fear of data misuse will not always be apparent but with government interference, whenever needed, and with access to the data only for beneficial purposes under strict laws and regulations, the possibility of misuse should shrink to a minimum. Additionally, if people realize that by sharing their data, without their names, can help someone close or far from them, they would happily accept it and cease to see themselves as a mere dot on a complex plot.

Moreover, skepticism among governments, universities and organizations independent of their size, should not exist about data sharing, if all regulations are followed, and ethics are a top priority, for a common, secure and transparent database system that will eventually benefit everyone.

Thus, ethics in data visualization have changed a lot in the last twenty years, with adaptations that now include more possible scenarios and take into consideration stricter regulations for individual security and privacy. However, further ethical challenges may arise in the near future with big data not only in health but also in other areas, which should be included in the data governance policy of each organization or government.

Breakthroughs, both in research and solutions to real-life problems can be accomplished if data from multiple resources are combined and protected under a common database system that prioritizes the ethics of each individual. Last but not least, if the "right to science" is more widely accepted and utilized unanimously, it may provide a better future for the generations to come.

ABOUT THE AUTHOR

Professor Hassan Ugail is the director of the Centre for Visual Computing at the University of Bradford in the UK. He is a mathematician and a renowned computer scientist in the area of visual computing and artificial intelligence. Data visualization is a key area he is actively studying and conducting research on.

https://en.wikipedia.org/wiki/Hassan_Ugail

tweet @ugail

https://www.facebook.com/ugail

www.ingramcontent.com/pod-product-compliance
Lightning Source LLC
LaVergne TN
LVHW051242050326
832903LV00028B/2519